CW00499544

Management from the Masters

Management from the Masters

From Confucius to Warren Buffett
Twenty Timeless Principles for Business

Morgen Witzel

B L O O M S B U R Y
LONDON • NEW DELHI • NEW YORK • SYDNEY

First published in Great Britain 2014

Copyright © Morgen Witzel, 2014

Bloomsbury Publishing Plc
50 Bedford Square
London
WC1B 3DP

www.bloomsbury.com

Bloomsbury Publishing
London, New Delhi, New York and Sydney

All rights reserved; no part of this publication may be reproduced, stored in a retrieval system, or transmitted by any means, electronic, mechanical, photocopying or otherwise, without the prior written permission of the Publisher.

No responsibility for loss caused to any individual or organisation acting or refraining from action as a result of the material in this publication can be accepted by Bloomsbury Publishing or the authors.

A CIP record for this book is available from the British Library.

ISBN: 9-781-472904751

10 9 8 7 6 5 4 3 2 1

Design by Fiona Pike, Pike Design, Winchester
Typeset by Hewer Text UK Ltd, Edinburgh
Printed and bound in Great Britain by CPI Group (UK) Ltd, Croydon CR0 4YY

Contents

About the Author

Morgen Witzel is a Fellow of the Centre for Leadership Studies at the University of Exeter Business School. He is the author of more than twenty books including the bestsellers *Tata: The Evolution of a Corporate Brand* and *Doing Business in China*. His books have been translated into 11 languages. His articles have appeared in the *Financial Times*, the *Los Angeles Times*, the *Toronto Globe and Mail*, *The Smart Manager*, *Financial World*, and many others.

Introduction

Management is a complex activity. It requires us to be able to think on many different levels and about many different things, often more than one at a time. The world is changing around us, often very quickly and often in ways we cannot see or anticipate. New communication technologies which were supposed to make our work easier, instead blitz us with more information than we can possibly make sense of or absorb. Globalisation opens up borders, creates new markets, and exposes us to a range of competitive challenges that did not exist a decade ago. Challenges to sustainability - climate change, looming shortages of fossil fuels and water, soil depletion and rising populations - are increasing the demands and pressures made on businesses from many different angles: new regulations, financial pressures, changing expectations and demands on the part of consumers, the media, and society as a whole. The job of the manager is without doubt getting harder, not easier.

Some managers cope with these pressures better than others. Some managers thrive in these difficult conditions while others struggle to make an impact, or fall by the wayside. Successful managers are those who can sense patterns and make connections that are not immediately obvious. They understand the relationships between productivity and the behaviour of employees, between profitability and customer relationships, between financial performance and effective management. Where others see contradictions and chaos, they see order. Where others see barriers and challenges, they see opportunities. They are the masters of complexity.

How do they do it? Successful managers realise that there are immutable laws in the world of management that influence almost every aspect. Understanding those laws and coming to terms with them makes all the difference between success and failure.

Some of these laws are part of the fabric of the universe. The law of entropy, the law of evolution, the law of unintended consequences

– these are not unique to businesses but affect all of us, everywhere. Some of these laws relate to personality, needs and behaviour, our ability to process knowledge, and what it means to be human and exist in a society with other people. Others relate to the dynamics of organisations, how we interact and work together in groups. All of them are equally important; many interconnect with each other.

This book presents 20 such laws. Each chapter covers one law, describing its origins and how it came about and, where appropriate, giving a brief history of its evolution and development. The impact of each law on management is explained, along with a description of the consequences should that law be broken, and the positive impacts that will accrue if the law is obeyed. Examples of companies that have obeyed – or broken – the law reinforce these points. We also see how some laws relate to and interconnect with other laws.

I have used the term 'law' rather loosely. These are not laws in the sense of jurisprudence. These laws are not written down as statutes. If you break them, there are no police or courts to enforce them. These are what philosophers term 'natural laws', inescapable and immutable forces rooted in physics, psychology, economics, and other disciplines. These are laws that no one can violate – at least, not for long. Breaking any of these laws will provoke an inevitable reaction by the natural forces behind each. Short-term transgressions may be possible, but in the long term nemesis will always catch up.

(This is true of 19 of the laws described in this book, but there is one exception. One of the laws presented here *must* be broken. There is a very high probability of negative consequences for you and for your organisation if it is not.)

My aim in writing this book is not to be prescriptive. I merely tell you what the laws are and make you aware of the consequences; if you want to break them, it is up to you. What I hope very much is that this book will stimulate you to think about management in new ways, and perhaps discuss these concepts with your colleagues. And surely, now of all times, we need to start thinking about management in new ways. We need to stop thinking that if we follow plans and tick boxes, everything will be fine and success will be waiting around the corner. The laws of management mean that we need to be able to work with complexity, with paradox, with human feelings and emotions, not just with numbers on a spreadsheet.

Management is complex, far more complex than most of us realise, and the laws of management mean that those complexities cannot be reduced. But if we understand them and master them, we can make them work for us.

Finally, under each law I have also included a selection of further readings, all of which are consolidated in the bibliography at the back of the book. These should enable you to learn more about the origins or effects of any given law.

The ancient philosopher Plato once remarked that good people do not need laws to tell them to act responsibly. A great deal of what you read in this book will sound like simple common sense, and indeed it is. But then, I have always held that simple common sense is one of the most valuable attributes of a manager (and also, in my experience, one of the most rare). I do not think that I am saying anything radical in this book; there are no heterodoxies, no unpalatable truths. Instead, what I hope you will find is a series of reminders of what is really important and necessary in management, together with a discussion of why this is so. We have had enough, over the past few years, of people trying to reinvent business and breaking the laws of management in the process. It is not just these people who have paid the price for the resulting failures; indirectly, we have all paid part of the price. It is time to get back to basics, time to return to the fundamentals of how management must be done. I hope this book will play a small part in reminding people of what those fundamentals are.

Part 1

The Laws of the Universe

We are strange folk, we business people, strange and sometimes a little arrogant. We often think that because we work in complex and powerful organisations that make a lot of money, we are somehow different, apart from the ordinary: we are clever, intelligent, and well- educated, and we have worked hard to achieve success; we are not ordinary people; we are exceptional, and because we are exceptional the ordinary rules of the universe do not apply to us; we are powerful and we can do anything we want to. This attitude was saturised brilliantly in Tom Wolfe's novel *The Bonfire of the Vanities*, in which the hero, a successful trader in the New York financial markets, described himself and his colleagues as 'Masters of the Universe'.

But the physical rules of the universe govern us all and we must accept this. More, if we know that this is true and understand how and why, we can turn this knowledge to our advantage.

First and foremost, we need to realise that time does not stand still. Things change constantly, even if imperceptibly. That does not mean the past is irrelevant: the past can be a powerful tool that helps us better understand the future. But we are all subject to time.

With time comes decay. The law of entropy tells us that decay is a constant and accelerating process. There is no such thing as a steady state. All around us the universe is crumbling into decay – even while it continues to expand. This applies to organisations and markets just as much as people. It is not enough to get to the peak, to achieve a position of market or technological dominance. Every competitive position, every business, every organisation contains within it the seeds of its own decay and ultimate destruction – unless steps are taken to counteract this decay.

And those steps *can* be taken because along with decay there is another form of change: evolution. The principles of evolution as described and elucidated by Charles Darwin, Herbert Spencer, Alfred Russel Wallace and others has also been shown to apply to markets and organisations. Evolved change is a form of response to external stimuli, no matter whether you are running a business or conducting a biological experiment. The business world is constantly changing and evolving in just this way, and only a fool would fail to recognise this. Again, there is a need to take steps to understand and match the evolution that we see around us. We too must evolve, because the only other option is stagnation and decline.

If we take these two examples, we find that we have a paradox. Decay and growth are happening simultaneously and are closely linked; how can this be so? To understand how the two processes are linked requires an understanding and acceptance of paradox. Chinese culture, through its concept of yin and yang, is very good at explaining paradox. Cartesian- oriented Western culture, with its emphasis on linear thinking, is not. India stands somewhere in the middle. But whatever their background, no manager will flourish unless he or she is capable of managing paradox, for paradox is one of the inescapable laws of the universe.

Management requires the making of decisions, but decisions are a bit like nuclear chain reactions. The consequences of our decisions impact on other people and things, with further consequences when those people and things react in ways that impact on other people and things, and so on. The law of unintended consequences reminds us that the decisions often have impacts and effects that we cannot anticipate. And since decisions cannot be unmade – we cannot go back against the flow of time – we have to live with those consequences. This, again, is inevitable; there is nothing we can do about this. We need to recognise the existence of the law of unintended consequences and make decisions carefully in the light of this knowledge.

The laws of the universe constrain what we can do as managers and leaders. By recognising these laws and paying heed to them, we stand a chance of making more realistic plans and decisions, as well as being better able to cope with uncertainty. We are part of the universe, and it is part of us. We should adapt our behaviour accordingly.

Chapter 1

The Law of Entropy (Time's Arrow)

The concept of entropy was formulated in the mid-nineteenth century by physicists including Ludwig Boltzmann and Rudolf Clausius, as part of the second law of thermodynamics. Put very simply, entropy is a measure of the amount of energy that escapes from or is not available to a given process. Consider, for example, a power station. The electricity generated by the station travels along power lines to the people who are to use it. During the course of transmission, depending on the length of the power lines, anywhere between 30 and 70 per cent of the electricity generated will be lost. That is what happens in any technical process. No matter how much energy is theoretically available, some of it will be lost.

The second law of thermodynamics tells us that within a given system, entropy increases over time. The energy that binds systems together slowly becomes weaker, and the systems themselves begin to decay. Astrophysicists tell us that this is true of the universe itself. Even though the universe is still expanding, the forces of entropy are increasing steadily. Eventually the universe will stop growing and then the entire system will begin to decay. Eventually everything – galaxies, stars, planets, all life and even atoms themselves – will no longer exist. In the words of astrophysicist Dr Brian Cox, 'Nothing will happen – and it will keep on not happening for a very, very long time'.

Although the modern theory of entropy dates, as I said, to about a century and a half ago, the concept has been known for much longer. Ancient Greek philosophers such as Empedocles and Heraclitus wrote about change and flux, and conceived the universe to be constantly changing with cycles of growth and decay. The ancient Hindu philosophical school known as Sankhya described the interrelationship between energy and inertia, which we can see as being a form of entropy. Buddhists and Jains were also aware of the process; the Jain concept of *aloka* and the Buddhist *nirvana* both referring to the state that exists after the decay of matter is complete.

There are several consequences of this. First, the increase in entropy means that time is a one-way process. In 1927 the astronomer Arthur Eddington described this concept as 'time's arrow'. Because the amount of energy available in any system – including the universe as a whole – is constantly decreasing and the amount of entropy is constantly increasing, it is impossible to go back in time. Second, the speed at which systems decay increases progressively. That is, once things start to decay, they do so more and more rapidly as they approach their final dissolution.

Rudolf Clausius used the following example, which anyone can see for themselves: take a glass, fill it with ice cubes, and leave it in a warm room. The ice cubes will start to melt, slowly at first, but then more and more quickly. The final few chunks of ice, swimming in warm water, will take no time at all to dissolve. What is more, once they have begun to dissolve the process is irreversible. The process of melting cannot be turned back and the ice cubes recreated.

Ah, you might say, but I can tip the water back into an ice cube tray, put it back in the freezer and re-freeze it once more. True, but that will not be a recreation of the original ice cubes. You will be using the same water, but you will be creating different ice cubes, and what is more, you will need a new input of energy (electricity to power the freezer) to make these new ice cubes.

Now take another example: take a fresh piece of fruit, a peach or a mango, and leave it on a table in a warm room. At first, nothing will appear to happen. Then slowly spots will appear; the fruit will become soft to the touch; and then very suddenly it will begin to rot. The process of decay will advance rapidly until you are left with nothing but a pool of smelly goo. And you cannot reverse this process. There is no way of reassembling the original fruit from the rotting mess you are left with. That is time's arrow at work.

So much for the lesson in science and philosophy, but what does this have to do with management? The answer is, everything. It is not just physical systems that decline as they lose energy. We can see exactly the same thing happening in human systems, including governments, societies, and business organisations. There are several consequences that we need to observe, including the impact of time's arrow on decisions, the influence of past decisions, and the broader impact of entropy on organisations over the course of time.

> The moving finger writes, and having writ
> Moves on: nor all thy piety nor wit
> Shall lure it back to cancel half a line
> Nor all thy tears wash out a word of it.
> –*Rubaiyat*, attributed to Omar Khayyam

The quote above, taken from Fitzgerald's famous translation of the *Rubaiyat*, is an elegant expression of the concept of time's arrow – what is done cannot be undone. Once an arrow is shot from a bow, it cannot be recalled – it continues on to its target. Every decision we make has consequences (not all of them intended, as we will see later in this book).

How often have we been in meetings or team discussions where, when options are being debated and someone says, 'Why don't we try this? If it doesn't work, we can always go back and start over?' How often have we heard about people who make mistakes 'reversing decisions' in order to put things right? The view that we can 'take back' or 're-make' a decision is widespread. But it is also a complete fallacy. Time's arrow tells us that we can never go back. A decision, once made, cannot be unmade. In order to get over the consequences of a wrong decision, rather than 'reversing' (which is physically impossible), we need instead to make a *new* decision which will have new consequences. And that new decision requires an input of resources and energy, just as re-freezing water to create a new tray of ice cubes will require new energy.

You may argue that if a company takes a decision to, say, introduce a new model of a car to its existing output, and then customers turn away from the offering, it can then cancel the decision, withdraw the model and go on as before. But a little consideration will show that this is not true. The decision to introduce the model exists; it always will exist. It is a fact. The decision to withdraw is a new and separate decision. And both of these decisions have consequences in terms of development and engineering time, managerial time, capital investment, and so on.

To repeat, every decision has consequences and we should always act as though those decisions and those consequences are cast in stone.

Because according to time's arrow, they are. We can no more 're-make' decisions than we can conjure up a new piece of fresh fruit out of the rotten mess of an old one.

The result of this is that every organisation – especially those that have existed for some time – is influenced by decisions that have been taken in the past. You could understand organisations as being the sum of all past decisions. What people decided to do in the past – including the wrong decisions as well as the right ones – helps to determine how the organisation works, thinks, and acts today. Economists refer to this as 'path dependence' or 'lock-in'. A common, simple example is the standard typewriter or computer keyboard, known as QWERTY by the first letters of the top row. The QWERTY keyboard is not the most efficient keyboard layout, as many studies have shown. Among other things it is left-hand dominant, making it more difficult for right-handed people to learn and use. But, it was the first standard keyboard layout and was widely adopted. Several generations of people have been trained to type in this way. What would be the cost of retraining people to use a different keyboard? Older people (like myself) probably couldn't manage it at all. So we go on with QWERTY, even though we know it is not the best system, because of decisions made in the past.

Why do the British drive on the left side of the road and the Europeans on the right? Because of choices made long in the past. Why do Indians drive on the left side of the road? Because India was part of the British empire. Suppose it were decided that it was more efficient to drive on the right – would it be possible to re-educate British and Indian drivers to switch? Maybe, but the process would be a very hard one.

Corporations are subject to path dependence too. In the late 1990s General Motors made a decision to invest heavily in sports-utility vehicles (SUVs). These are large and heavy automobiles that consume a great deal of fuel. At the time, demand for these cars was high and fuel prices low. By 2006, though, fuel prices had soared, even in America, and demand was collapsing. Yet General Motors was stuck on a course to which it had been committed by decisions made 10 years earlier. What were the choices? Go back? But time's arrow made that impossible. Stick to the path it had chosen and continue to make SUVs? Or make a new decision to scale down SUVs and go in a new direction (compact cars, hybrids, etc.)? So set was General Motors in its way that it continued on its course. In 2008 the company declared bankruptcy, and only when it was almost too late did General Motors set about changing course.

General Motors had, to some extent, been a victim of its own success. It was the world's largest automobile maker, and had been for many decades since the end of the 1920s. It thought it was invulnerable. But the broader implication of the law of entropy is that everything decays, and that applies to markets and competitive positions as well as physical systems. We can think of many others. In the 1990s, Motorola regarded itself as the impregnable giant of the mobile phone technology. Completely path dependent on analog technology, Motorola watched its competitive position decay as digital technology took hold and new competitors such as Nokia rose to the fore. Then Nokia became dominant, and more than a decade later *its* competitive position is eroding with ever-increasing speed as smartphones take over the market.

Think of Tesco, the world's largest retailer, once beloved of investors and hailed as a pioneer of e-commerce. Now everyone is doing e-commerce, Tesco's shops which were once the epitome of modernity look tired; its product lines are dated and its competitors are undercutting it on price. Think of Infosys. Once hailed as the shining example of the modern Indian company its star is now fading and its brand declining. Ten years ago it was almost inconceivable that people should criticise Infosys for falling behind. Now its critics are lining up to have a go.

There is sometimes an apparent relationship between entropy and path dependence, as we saw in the cases of General Motors and Motorola. Companies become wedded to a particular technology and, as Clayton Christensen described in *The Innovators' Dilemma*, they refuse to consider the possibility of relinquishing that technology in favour of something new. But even where path dependence is less of a problem, entropy still occurs. Kodak, the world leader in photographic film production, did try to adapt to the age of digital photography but failed. There were a variety of reasons for this but complacency certainly played a role. Kodak waited until the heyday of its innovation was past before trying to create something new. Christensen and others tell us that waiting so long can be fatal. The time to start thinking about the next innovation is shortly after the previous one has been launched.

Can entropy be overcome? In the long, cosmological frame of time, the answer would appear to be 'no'. Physicists tell us that the universe is bound to decay in the end. But for the purposes of our own life and our world, there are solutions. The first is to make sure that a system remains dynamic. So long as it is capable of growth, or at least of managing change, the forces of entropy can be counteracted. It used to be thought that there was such a thing as a corporate life cycle, that corporations were born, grew, declined, and died just as living creatures do. However, Charles Baden-Fuller and John Stopford's *Rejuvenating the Mature Firm* has shown that this is not necessarily so. Injections of fresh energy - capital, technology, creative brain-power, and imagination - can turn companies around, help them to rebuild and grow once more.

Nor is path dependence inevitable. Nokia transformed itself from a forest products company to a mobile phone maker; Kao branched out from chemicals into computer disks; Tata expanded from a heavy industrial base to high technology and services. Again, what is required is an injection of fresh resources and, above all, fresh thinking.

However, it is vital to recognise that entropy always exists. It cannot be beaten. The struggle against the forces of entropy is constant and ongoing, and companies and managers must be constantly on their guard against it. The moment they lower their guard, the moment they become complacent, decay begins.

Further Reading:

Arthur, W. Brian (1994) *Increasing Returns and Path Dependence in the Economy*, Ann Arbor, Michigan: University of Michigan Press.

Baden-Fuller, Charles and Stopford, John (1992) *Rejuvenating the Mature Business*, London: Routledge.

Carroll, Sean (2011) *From Eternity to Here: The Quest for the Ultimate Theory of Time*, New York: Oneworld Publications.

Christensen, Clayton (1997) *The Innovator's Dilemma: When New Technologies Cause Great Firms to Fail*, Boston: Harvard Business School Press.

Kloetzli, R. (2004) *Buddhist Cosmology: From Single World System to Pure Land*, Delhi: Motilal Banarsidass.

Penrose, Roger (2005) *The Road to Reality: A Complete Guide to the Laws of the Universe*, New York: Alfred A. Knopf.

Chapter 2

Darwin's Rule

Darwin's rule is this: it is not the strongest that survive, nor the most intelligent, but those that are best capable of adaptation.

Charles Darwin, one of the founders of modern evolutionary theory, has had a more profound impact on our thinking about science and society than almost any other person living or dead. Not everyone accepts the theory of evolution, and some campaign actively against it, usually on religious grounds. But whatever one's views on creation and the origin of the world, Darwin and his colleagues discovered something profound which cannot be denied. Organisms adapt and change as they interact with each other and in response to pressures in their environment. We can see this all around us in the world today. We can see this in ourselves.

Darwin's first insights came during a voyage of exploration in the South Pacific in the 1830s. In the Galapagos Islands, he noticed how some species had evolved distinctive characteristics that were not found elsewhere. These variations within species were hard to explain given the existing theories of biology. Darwin came to the conclusion that species must evolve and change over time. He put this down to competition between organisms for scarce resources. Some life forms adapt in ways that allow them to use resources more effectively (an example might be early humans learning to use tools and create fire). These are the species that tend to become dominant. Those that fail to evolve fall behind and are either dominated or perish entirely.

The notion of competition was taken up in particular by Herbert Spencer, who helped to develop the theory of 'social Darwinism', which opined that certain people were better adapted to survive and succeed. Others went on to apply this theory to business, and there was a strong influence on modern free market theory. Throw open the doors to competition, the argument came from economists of the Chicago School and the Austrian School; the companies that are the fittest will succeed, the weak companies will fall by the wayside – and that is as it should be.

This idea that 'the strong will live and the weak will perish' is a common perception of Darwinism, but this is quite wrong. As Darwin himself said, it is not the strongest that survive, or the most intelligent, but those best able to adapt and evolve. In other words, neither brute strength nor cleverness is a guarantee of success.

As Geoffrey Hodgson and Thorbjørn Knudsen pointed out in their book *Darwin's Conjecture*, there is much more to Darwinism than competition. Other key concepts in the theory of evolution include:

- **Mutual aid**, the process by which species offer each other support to overcome problems.

  The Russian philosopher Prince Peter Kropotkin picked up on this idea and developed it further, arguing that in human terms, most of the great advances of civilisation have come about through human beings collaborating in a common cause, rather than competing. In our own time we can think of great collaborative projects, for example, Bluetooth.
- **Sympathy or 'fellow feeling'**, which can be seen in animals as well as humans.

  Many species will look after and protect weaker members of their group rather than letting them perish, and this trait is also noticeable in human development; charity is one of the great attributes of civilization;
- **Cooperation**, similar to mutual aid but referring particularly to the process whereby members of the same species work together to achieve a common goal.

  We can think of how lions hunt, or how buffalo unite to form defensive circles against a threat. People do the same; the first organisations in human society, families, and tribes, emerged out of a realisation that people working together can achieve more than they can working alone. Our modern organisations are still based on this same principle.

Another leading figure of early evolutionary theory, Alfred Russel Wallace, argued (and Darwin agreed) that the most important pressures that led to evolution came not from competition between individuals or between species, but from environmental pressures. When the environment changes, Wallace argued, species and organisms must change too in order to adapt to the new conditions. If they fail to do so they might run out of food or be hunted to extinction by other species. This happens at every level. Some of the most rapidly adaptable organisms in the world today are viruses, which are constantly mutating, faster than scientists can develop antiviral drugs to deal with them.

The law of entropy, discussed in the previous chapter, tells us that there will always be change. It follows that a constant adaptation is necessary in order to keep up with change. The natural world knows this, and animals and plants are evolving all the time, even if those evolutionary changes are not always visible to the eye. So, what relevance does this have for modern management?

As we said in the last chapter, the laws that we observe in the natural world are at play in society as well. It is easy to observe how businesses behave according to the laws of evolution. They compete, but they also engage in mutual support, and every organisation depends on cooperation among its members. They respond to their environment and change and adapt according to environmental pressures.

People have been thinking about businesses as equivalents to life forms for a long time. The medieval Christian philosopher John of Salisbury thought that organisations were like human beings, with heads (the brain that guides and controls the organisation), hearts (the motivating spirit and values), and arms and legs (the active parts that do the labour the organisation needs). The nineteenth-century British chemist Andrew Ure wrote on very similar lines. In the early twentieth century, the American engineer Harrington Emerson, strongly influenced by Darwin, described at length how businesses adapt to their environment in the same way that animals and plants do, and also argued for the presence of mutual support between businesses.

The economist Kenneth Boulding, in his book *The Image*, set out the view that organisations can be perceived on seven different levels:

1 **The static level:** a snapshot of the organisation as it is at a given moment.
2 **The clockwork dynamic level:** the organisation as a machine with moving parts all working together but in a mindless fashion (and subject to entropy).

3 **The level of 'homeostatic control':** the organisation has communications systems and feedback devices which enable it to maintain a working equilibrium.
4 **The biological level:** the organisation is made up of self-maintaining cells.
5 **The botanical level:** the same, only with some cells taking different forms from others according to the functions they serve, their combined functions serving to support life and growth.
6 **The animal level:** the organisation is a living organism capable of movement, awareness, and reaction.
7 **The human level:** as above, but the organisation also has the power of conscious thought, self-consciousness, and self-awareness.

Thus, there is plenty of evidence that businesses adapt and evolve just as plants and animals do. But, the critical point to recognise here is the extra level that Boulding adds, the human level. We, too, adapt and evolve; but because we have conscious thought and self-awareness, we *know* that we need to adapt in order to survive. So, we need to return to Darwin's Rule. Neither brain nor brawn is sufficient to help us on their own. To survive, our businesses must be capable of adaptation. What does that mean exactly?

In his book *Changeability*, London Business School professor Michael Jarrett analysed the responses of companies to the need for change. Jarrett grouped companies into three classes. First, there are the *avoiders* of change. These, like the captain of the *Titanic*, refuse to recognise the need for change even when it stares them in the face. These are least capable of adaptation. Next come the *analysts*. These are very good at spotting change in the environment, but less clear about how to go about adapting. Sometimes they fall prey to 'analysis paralysis' and get stuck on evaluating options without making a decision; sometimes they are frightened to take risks. Finally there are the *adapters*, who are ready to take change and are even proactive about doing so.

What sets the adapters apart from the others? Jarrett believes there are three essential factors: awareness of the changes in the environment; internal capacity for change; and leadership to ensure that change is followed through. In terms of internal capabilities he identifies five in particular:

- **Scanning the horizon:** frequent and deliberate 'radar screen' sweeps of what is going on around the company;
- **Making sense of the signs:** the ability to understand and interpret the blips that show up on that radar screen;
- **Creating a culture of openness:** where people are encouraged to share information about perceived threats and work together to meet them (sympathy, cooperation);
- **Weighing in the anchors of dysfunctional routine:** or in other words, getting rid of the internal barriers and resistance to change;
- **Fluid execution:** fast response to change and implementation of change programmes.

The ability to respond to change which Darwin says is essential to survival is not something that comes naturally. It has to be worked for; it must be built into the organisation as a matter of deliberate policy. Here is an example which shows how it can be done:

The Tata group, despite its long and admired history and traditions, had reached a difficult point by the late 1980s. Its long-time leader, the great J.R.D. Tata, was now in the twilight of his years and his powers were fading. His senior executives were now concentrating less on the business and more on which of them would have the right to succeed him. New ideas were not emerging and there was no growth. The group's reputation was slipping too; as one observer said at the time, Tata was loved and admired rather than respected. The Tata image among young people in particular had begun to weaken. In short, entropy had set in.

In 1991 J.R.D. handed over to Ratan Tata, who at once began to renew the process of evolution. Ratan Tata knew that Tata needed to become a more international company in response to globalisation and the opening up of the Indian economy. He also knew that the company had to become more adaptable and better able to change. He thus demonstrated awareness of changes in the external environment and the need for internal capabilities, and he provided the leadership. Over the course of 20 years, Ratan Tata turned the Tata group into a modern business enterprise, multinational in focus and with global aspirations; he oversaw its growth and expansion into new markets, built a strong brand which appealed to all segments of society, and introduced stronger mechanisms for internal coordination. Tata evolved in response to the new business environment, to the point where it is ranked today as one of the top fifty global brands by value, and in 2008 was rated one of the 10 most innovative businesses in the world.

Ratan Tata knew that if he did nothing, entropy would continue and the group would decay at a faster and faster rate. He gave Tata the capacity to evolve and change and showed how a mature firm could be rejuvenated and how entropy (temporarily at least) could be beaten.

Evolution is a force we cannot ignore. Darwin was right: adapters will succeed, avoiders will fail. It is up to us to choose which we will be.

Further Reading:

Bateson, Gregory (1988) *Mind and Nature: A Necessary Unity*, New York: Bantam.

Boulding, Kenneth (1956) *The Image*, Ann Arbor: University of Michigan Press.

Darwin, Charles (2006) *On the Origin of Species by Means of Natural Selection*, Mineola, NY: Dover.

Hodgson, Geoffrey and Knudsen, Thorbjørn (2010) *Darwin's Conjecture: The Search for General Principles of Social and Scientific Evolution*, Chicago: University of Chicago Press.

Jarrett, Michael (2009) *Changeability: Why Some Companies are Ready for Change – And Others Aren't*, London: FT-Prentice Hall.

Kropotkin, Peter (1976) *Mutual Aid: A Factor of Evolution*, New York: Sargent.

Wallace, Alfred Russel (2008) *Darwinism*, New York: Macmillan.

Chapter 3

The Rule of Yin and Yang

Properly speaking, yin and yang itself is not a rule. It is a concept derived from ancient Chinese philosophy, particularly from Daoism (or Taoism). In Chapter 42 of the Daoist classic *Daodejing*, yin and yang are described as the 'vital breaths' from which all things 'derive their harmony'. We can think of yin and yang as being the elemental forces that bind the universe together, rather like atoms.

Yin and *yang* literally mean 'light' and 'dark' and this has mistakenly led some, particularly in the West, to think of the two as polar opposites. In fact they are closely interlinked. Think of the daily cycle of sunrise and sunset, of how light gives way to darkness which in turn gives way to light again. So long as the earth rotates on its axis, we will continue to have both light *and* dark. Indeed, the proper transliteration of the Chinese characters is not yin *and* yang but yin-yang, or literally, 'light-dark', indicating that the two are parts of a single entity.

The concept of yin and yang can be applied to many facets of the world around us. Think of winter and summer; each is part of the yearly cycle, and you cannot have one without the other. Think of male and female: seemingly opposite concepts, yet in fact each depending on the other. Think of waves on the sea, with high crests of waves and low troughs between them, all forming part of the same pattern of rolling waves.

Think, too, of planting a seed in the ground. Watered and with access to light and heat, the seed will sprout and grow upwards. Then, at the end of the growing season, it will decay and collapse back to the ground, eventually rotting and being swallowed up in the soil from which it had grown. There is a yin and yang cycle, say the Daoists, of growth and decay that goes on continuously in the world around us – and indeed in ourselves, in our own bodies and minds.

This conjoining of the forces of growth and the forces of decay in a single model helps us to unite the concepts discussed in the previous two chapters, namely entropy (decay) and evolution (growth), but that is not our primary purpose here. Instead, we are going to use yin and yang to explore the concept of paradox.

A paradox is a statement (or statements) that lead to a conclusion that either contradicts the statements themselves, or simply does not make sense. Consider the following statement: 'All men are liars'. If the statement is true, and the person saying this is a man, then we have a logical problem. The man making this statement must also therefore be a liar, in which case what he says must be false and we are led to the conclusion that not all men are liars. Ah, we can say, in that case the statement must have been false all along. But that merely proves the point the statement is making, that men are liars, and therefore it must be true!

This is, of course, a mere semantic example (it is the sort of problem that philosophers spend hours debating and discussing) but it exposes a deeper problem. How do we deal with irreconcilable statements? Let us go back to our example of light and dark. How can a thing be both light and dark at the same time? The idea of being simultaneously in light and in dark seems impossible. But if we take the Daoist view, we realise that the world itself is both light and dark at the same time. The next time you take a long journey by air, look at the world maps which most airlines now use to display the position of the plane by GPS. Note how part of the world is in light and part is in dark; and although the position of light and dark change as the world rotates, the basic point that the world is both light and dark is always true.

Paradoxes are often a matter of perception. We *think* there is a paradox (as in the case of light and dark) where in fact no contradiction exists. The world around us is in both light and darkness at the same time. It is growing and decaying at the same time.

The rule of paradox, then, is this: we are surrounded by paradoxes everywhere; in the physical world, in the business world, in our organisations, in our own lives. In his book *The Hungry Spirit*, Charles Handy argues that paradox is 'inevitable, endemic and perpetual. The more turbulent the times, the more complex the world, the more the paradoxes.' If we accept this – as we must – then we have a choice. We can either break our necks trying to 'solve' each paradox we encounter and adopt the position that one pole is 'right' and the other is 'wrong' (i.e. light is better than dark, growth is better than decay, etc.) or we can accept the whole paradox and find ways of working with it. If we can do the latter more often, as in the case of light and darkness, it eventually turns out that there is no contradiction at all.

The *Daodejing* offers us a number of examples of paradoxes that affect human affairs. One famous one concerns the rule of kingdoms. How should states best be governed? Government suggests constraint and control, and this is directly opposed to the principle of personal free will, that people know best what is good for themselves. The *Daodejing* presents this paradox by maintaining that good government and personal freedom are two halves of the same whole. The best form of rule, in the end, is a rule so light and unburdensome that people hardly notice it. Trying to control people by giving them orders and directing their efforts, paradoxically, leads to inefficiency and confusion. Letting people do what they wish to do results in peace and order:

The highest type of ruler is one of whose existence the people are barely aware.

Next comes one whom they love and praise.

Next comes one whom they fear.

Next comes one whom they despise and defy.

Governance, say the Daoists, is an example of another paradox, that of 'less equals more'. That is, the lighter the hand of governance – in all organisations, including businesses – the more effective the organisation becomes.

There are plenty of examples of paradox in the world of business. Take for example the problem of efficiency and effectiveness. Ask many people, including many managers, and they will tell you that the most efficient business is also the most effective. That is not necessarily so. An efficient train service, for example, might be one where 100 per cent of seats are filled on every train. But would this be effective? Passengers might be so crammed together that they are uncomfortable and finish their journeys tired and unhappy. Others might not get seats at all and be turned away. Both groups will be dissatisfied and might look for alternative forms of transport for their next journey. In the long run, this lack of effectiveness – in terms of passenger satisfaction – could lead to dwindling passenger numbers and thus a loss of efficiency. Similarly, hotel owners know that a hotel that is fully booked all of the time is actually a cause of dissatisfaction among customers who turn up at the last minute hoping for a room. In America, hotels regard 93-95 per cent advance bookings as about optimum, even though this means there might be empty rooms, which is technically inefficient.

The problem becomes even more serious when we look at hospitals. If a hospital is entirely full, all of the time, then there is no room for new patients to be admitted. Seriously ill patients might not receive the treatment they need, and some might die. Hospitals must have beds, and by implication medical staff, standing by in case they are needed but not actually work. This is inefficient but it is effective and saves lives.

Another paradox in the business world is that of regulation and competition. These are usually seen as polar opposites. I have listened many times to my MBA students complain that regulation is hurting their own businesses, making it harder to employ people, and cutting into profitability. But if we take the Daoist view that regulation and competition are two halves of the same coin - that the ultimate purpose of regulation is, or should be, the creation of a free market where everyone including customers, employees, and shareholders is created fairly - then we can begin to see that (most) regulation does make sense.

And once we have taken that step, it is a short further step to turning law and regulation to competitive advantage. In their book *Proactive Law for Managers*, George Siedel and Helena Haapio argue that companies which comply with the law will always have a competitive advantage over those that do not; and further, that companies which comply early with new laws will gain advantage over those that lag behind. But the real winners, they say, are those that engage with the regulatory process and assist in the formation and implementation of regulations. These will always win advantage over those that fight against legislation or try to avoid it.

A related paradox can be found in many parts of the world namely the paradox of corruption. Almost everyone knows that corruption is wrong, and almost everyone is aware of the damaging effects of corruption on society and on the individual mind and spirit. Yet people continue to pay bribes. Each time they do so, according to the law of entropy, they make an already bad situation a little worse by reinforcing the culture of corruption and making it harder to break the cycle. Paradoxically, if people stopped paying bribes corruption would wither up and die.

Yet another common paradox in business is the paradox of profit and growth. It is received wisdom that companies can concentrate on high profitability or on high growth – they cannot do both at once. Bala Chakravarthy and Peter Lorange in their book *Profit or Growth* found that fewer than 5 per cent of large companies managed to both make profits and sustain growth over the long term (in their study, a period of 10 years). They found an underlying tension between growth, which involves entrepreneurial behaviour and risk-taking in order to expand into new markets, and profitability, which requires concentration on the current position in order to achieve profits: 'competing for the future obliges a company to risk the present'. However, they also found that there was a paradox: growth without profitability leads in the end to financial crisis and even bankruptcy, as companies such as Nortel and Royal Ahold have discovered. And profitability without growth leads to stagnation and entropy, as we saw earlier with Kodak and Motorola.

Chakravarthy and Lorange realised that we need a business model which allows us to focus on both profitability and growth at the same time. They looked at the 5 per cent that manage both, companies such as Nestlé and American retailer Best Buy (they did not consider the Tata group, though it certainly fits into this category). They found that in these companies there is a process of 'continuous renewal' as the company constantly shifts and adjusts its position to take advantage of new opportunities for profit, thereby avoiding being bogged down in Christensen's 'innovator's dilemma'. Growth is not for its own sake; growth is clearly targeted at opportunities for achieving higher profits. But this, for many executives, still represents a paradox.

Charles Handy gives nine paradoxes which he believes affect everyone, business people included, in the world today. Briefly summarised, these are:

1 **The paradox of intelligence.** Brainpower, not muscle power, is the new source of productive wealth. But it is harder to control people's

minds, and the unpredictability of human behaviour means that this powerful source of wealth can also be the most risky to use and work with.

2 **The paradox of work.** Pay for people at the top end of the scale is rising steadily, while pay for those at the bottom end is stagnant or declining in real terms.
3 **The paradox of productivity.** Fewer and fewer people are responsible for an ever-increasing share of global productivity.
4 **The paradox of time.** The paradoxes of work and productivity means that most of us have less time available to use for our own ends. People are working longer and longer hours, often without seeing any real rise in their standard of living.
5 **The paradox of riches.** The world is wealthier today than at any time in history, but there has been no corresponding increase in human happiness. Indeed, there is no evidence that even the very wealthy are particularly happy. Is Paris Hilton happier than a road sweeper?
6 **The paradox of organisations.** Increasingly businesses have to focus simultaneously on mass markets and niches, to be global *and* local at the same time.
7 **The paradox of age.** People's values change as they age, and the values of the elderly and those of the young are often at odds with each other.
8 **The paradox of the individual.** We are all individuals and have our own personalities and our own needs; yet, as we shall see when we come to discuss Maslow's hierarchy of needs (Chapter 5), we all need things from others and we all stand as part of a group, or groups.
9 **The paradox of justice.** The whole concept of justice depends on equity and fairness for all, and yet it is easy to look at the world around us and see how clearly injustices remain.

Handy is writing here in global, social terms, but the same paradoxes occur in businesses too. The Pareto principle (see Chapter 11) tells us that within organisations the greater part of productive value is achieved by a few people. People within organisations fight a constant battle to maintain their self-identity against the demands of others. Long-serving managers and new hires will clash over values and policy, and so on. It is easy to find analogues for all nine paradoxes within any organisation.

As Handy says, paradoxes are inevitable, endemic and perpetual. We cannot resist this fact; like the paradox of decay and growth, it is one of the inevitable laws of the universe. We are best served by taking the advice of the Daoists, recognising this fact, and then working to understand paradoxes and determine how we can use that understanding to our best advantage.

Further Reading:

Chakravarthy, Bala and Lorange, Peter (2008) *Profit or Growth? Why You Don't Have to Choose*, Upper Saddle River, NJ: Wharton School Publishing.

Handy, Charles (1995) *The Empty Raincoat: Making Sense of the Future*, London: Arrow.

Hughes, Patrick and Brecht, George (1975) *Vicious Circles and Infinity: A Panoply of Paradoxes*, Garden City, NY: Doubleday.

Lao Tzu (1990), *Daodejing* (*Tao Teh Ching*), Boston: Shambhala.

Siedel, George and Haapio, Helena (2010) *Proactive Law for Managers*, Farnham: Gower.

Chapter 4

The Law of Unintended Consequences

The law of unintended consequences is exactly what its title suggests: decisions and actions have consequences that are not what the person making the decision or taking the action intended. We take a decision intending to get result A, and instead we get result B, which we did not intend; or perhaps we get both A and B, and the confluence of these leads to result C, which we did not intend either.

The basic concept has been known and discussed for a long time. In 1692 the English economist and philosopher John Locke argued against legislation to cut interest rates, which was intended to help borrowers get money more cheaply. In fact, said Locke, the bill would hurt borrowers as lenders would no longer be willing to lend at such low rates and the amount of money available for loans would dry up. In Britain at the time of writing, exactly this problem is affecting small businesses and home buyers; historically low interest rates means that there is a dearth of money available for loans, and lenders are not willing to take risks for such small returns.

Adam Smith's famous concept of the 'invisible hand' is another example of the law of unintended consequences, this time with beneficial effect. Smith argued that all of us, as economic actors, act in our own self-interest. We make purchases of goods and services that will enhance our own lives. In making purchases, we put money into circulation which supports the economy, providing employment for others and enabling them to make purchases too. The effect of our combined self-interest is to increase the well-being of others, and of society as a whole (astute readers will have spotted the paradox here).

Another economist, Frédéric Bastiat, believed that economists need to make distinctions between consequences of actions that are seen and those that are unseen, equivalent to our distinction between intended and unintended. His strongly expressed view was that economists – and

I would argue that this means all of us, as we are all economic actors whether we know it or not - need to be careful to take account of the unseen/unintended consequences. Belief that every decision or action will yield the result, and only the result, that is expected is erroneous. Rarely does this actually happen.

Indeed another scientific theory, chaos theory, argues that this *never* happens, that decisions *always* have unintended consequences, as in the famous example of a butterfly flapping its wings causing, through a chain of unintended consequences, a typhoon halfway around the world. There is not space to go deeply into chaos theory here, but one of its tenets is that complexity, like paradoxes and entropy, is increasing steadily as time's arrow moves forward. Thus the number of unintended consequences from each decision or action is increasing all the time.

The sociologist Robert K. Merton was the first to apply the principles of the law of unintended consequences to social situations, including organisations. Merton asked why decisions and actions have unintended consequences and came up with five reasons:

1 **Ignorance:** People do not have enough information at their disposal when they take the decision, and factors of which they were not previously aware skew the result so that the decision does not give the effect desired.
2 **Error:** People make the wrong decisions for the wrong reasons (perhaps as a result of ignorance).
3 **Immediacy of interest:** People realise that unintended consequences exist but choose to ignore these, calculating that their own interests will be served by the decision while the burden of the unintended consequences will be borne by others. A company that chooses to dump toxic material into a river in order to save on the costs of safe disposal, knowing that the health of villagers down the river will be affected, is behaving according to immediacy of interest.
4 **Basic values:** People act according to pre-conceived notions of how they should act, regardless of the consequences. Left-wing governments raise taxes and increase public spending in accordance with their basic values concerning redistribution of wealth, regardless of the unintended effects this might have in terms of flight of capital and rising costs of borrowing; right-wing governments slash public

spending and decrease taxes regardless of the effect this might have on employment and revenue generation.

5 **Self-defeating prophecies:** People anticipate unintended consequences and ward them off. Merton's example concerned the early nineteenth-century predictions of Malthus and others that increasing populations could result in a shortage of food and mass starvation. Alerted to this, scientists made advances in agricultural productivity that greatly increased food production and warded off the crisis. Today, more than 75 years since Merton was writing, we can note unintended consequences of this action: the great increase in agricultural production has had impacts including pollution from pesticides and burning, loss of biodiversity, and depletion of groundwater resources. None of these things were anticipated by the agricultural scientists of the nineteenth century.

Sometimes unintended consequences are positive in nature. Aspirin was originally developed by the Bayer company as a painkiller, but has since been found to be useful in preventing potential heart attacks and is now being investigated as a possible anti-cancer agent. The Japanese chemicals company Kao found that a chemical by-product of one of its production processes, which the company had been throwing away as worthless, was in fact a key component in the production of computer floppy disks. Kao branched out into floppy disk production, and within a year was the world leader in the market.

All too often, though, unintended consequences have negative impacts which affect the original decision-maker, other people around them, or both. One of the most famous instances took place in America in the 1920s. In order to combat alcoholism and crimes committed under the influence of alcohol, the government banned the production and sale of alcoholic beverages. The trade in alcohol went underground and was a major contributory factor in the rise of organised crime in America, a problem which still persists today long after alcohol was legalised again. Debates about the prohibition and criminalisation of certain types of recreational drugs often centre around the likelihood of similar unintended consequences.

The law of unintended consequences is a constantly occurring feature in the world of business. One contributing factor is the inability of many in the business world to accept the concept of paradox. Consider again what we said in the previous chapter about the paradox of efficiency and effectiveness, and how a system which is technically and financially efficient may in fact be ineffective when it comes to creating and delivering value to customers.

In the mid-1990s, Delta Airlines was one of the most successful airlines in America. Surveys regularly placed it at the top or near the top of league tables for customer satisfaction. Its staff was famous for their hospitality and their sunny smiles. For staff, nothing was too much trouble for their customers, and customers responded warmly by flying with the airline over and over again. This customer loyalty enabled the airline to get through the turbulent period in American aviation following the deregulation of the airline industry in 1978.

Then the chief executive of Delta retired and a new leader and a new team came in. Anticipating further difficulties in the airline industry, the new team decided on a self-defeating prophecy: they began cutting costs across the board, including wages and benefits paid to staff. The morale of the once friendly and motivated staff at Delta began to suffer. They stopped smiling and became less focused on customer care. Customers noticed this too. As service quality slid, customers began looking around and found that other airlines were now offering equal quality for better prices. Delta's passenger numbers and revenues slid and slid, until the company was forced to file for bankruptcy. Eventually the company came out of bankruptcy and is now striving to regain its former position but the last decade has been 10 lost years for Delta. None of this was intended when the original decision to cut costs was taken.

We have no choice but to accept that unintended consequences occur. Economists and physicists alike have proven their existence; common sense and experience tell us the same. Frédéric Bastiat's advice, that we need to always take account of the unintended consequences of decisions and actions, remains as valid now as when it was written in 1850. We need to do everything we can to work out in advance what the consequences of decisions will be and anticipate how we will deal with them when the time comes. Of course, there is no way of predicting the future so we cannot always get it right and a degree of 'organisational paranoia' will always be there (see Grove's Rule, Chapter 9). But we cannot simply bury our heads in the sand and assume that what we hope is going to happen *will* happen, or that it is *all* that will happen. Otherwise, like Delta, we will find our decisions coming back to bite us.

Further Reading:

Bastiat, Frédéric (1850) *That Which Is Seen, and That Which Is Not Seen*, http://bastiat.org/ en/twisatwins.html.

Bird, Richard J. (2003) *Chaos and Life: Complexity and Order in Evolution and Thought*, Columbia: Columbia University Press.

Merton, Robert K. (1936) 'The Unanticipated Consequences of Purposive Social Action', *American Sociological Review*, in Merton, *Sociological Ambivalence and Other Essays*, New York: Free Press, 1976.

Part 2
The Laws of Human Behaviour

Business is a social activity, and businesses are part of society. Despite all the high technology, the wireless broadband, the manufacturing robots and so on, the people who conduct business are human. Companies are staffed by human beings; they are directed and led by human beings; their customers are human beings, and even if their shareholders appear to be big faceless companies, those companies, too, are made up of human beings.

This means that we cannot ignore the complexities of human behaviour and, in particular, we cannot ignore the fact that human behaviour is often seemingly irrational and unpredictable. Economics, as it is conventionally taught today, tends to assume that people are rational agents and always act, as Adam Smith assumes, in their own self-interest. Heterodox economic thinkers such as behavioural economists, who attempt to bring together the principles of psychology and economics, have tried to modify this position, though so far with little success.

Economists working primarily with theoretical models may find it convenient to set the principles of human behaviour to one side in their quest for better understanding of how economic activity takes place. But those of us tasked with running businesses cannot afford to do so. It may be that in the very long term, over a century or so, human behaviour makes little difference to how economies perform. But businesses run with much shorter time horizons: 10 to 20 years for Chinese and Indian firms; five, three, or even two years for many European and American companies. They have to take account of human behaviour, human inconsistency, human frailties. Indeed, as marketing theory tells us, it is in the very lack of consistency of human behaviour that firms can often find competitive advantage.

One of the most powerful psychological theories of human behaviour, often cited by those attempting to explain behaviour in both the workplace and the marketplace, is the hierarchy of needs, first devised by Abraham Maslow. Although there are plenty of other theories of human behaviour, and Maslow's theory is not without its criticism, I have given Maslow's theory the status of 'law' because it cannot be ignored. No matter how one reformulates or reconceptualises it, the basic principle that human activity is driven by need, and that human needs change according to time and circumstance, remains universally true and valid. I have chosen Maslow's theory to represent this law because I find it simple, elegant, and easy to use. You may of course explore other theories of behaviour; in fact, I encourage you to do so.

Confucius's Golden Rule is another universally valid principle, which finds one of its earliest expressions in ancient China but has been conceptualised by most cultures in different ways. The idea that we should treat others as we wish to be treated ourselves is not just an ethical precept; it is one of the bedrocks of the concepts of equity and justice, which in turn are foundation stones of civilisation. As we are seeing at the time of writing in the Arab Spring in Egypt, Libya, and Syria, once the principles of equity and justice are violated then organisations - even society itself - are fatally compromised.

It is not enough for a society to be equitable and fair. As the ancient Indian sage Kautilya observed, the root of wealth is activity. We cannot simply sit and let a comfortable life and good things fall into our hands; we have to work for them. Kautilya's observation has implications for the nature of work and also the purpose of leadership. How we conceive of the relationship between activity and work on the one hand, and wealth and value on the other, is fundamental to business success.

Wealth and activity may be linked, but not all activity leads to wealth. Over the past few years we have seen how bad judgement and poor knowledge have led banks and other investors to take investment decisions that have had serious unintended consequences; in some cases, such as Lehman Brothers, those consequences have included their own collapse.

The legendary American investor Warren Buffett's dictum, 'Never invest in something you do not understand', has implications far beyond banking and investment. This law needs to be heeded by anyone, anywhere in management. We saw in Chapter 4 how many decisions with unintended consequences are the result of the lack of knowledge and lack of consideration for what the consequences might be. Buffett's Rule reminds us of the importance of advance knowledge.

Finally, again as we saw in Chapter 4, it is impossible to foresee every circumstance. Businesses can spread themselves very thin by trying to cover every potential problem and creating a number of self-defeating prophecies as they do so. But they will never be entirely safe, for there is always the risk of something not foreseen coming up on the blind side. Grove's Rule reminds us of the need for flexibility and adaptability; without these traits, success is at best problematic, at worst highly unlikely.

Understanding human behaviour requires us to accept that we as people do not always conform to the laws of economics (a factor which renders many of those laws invalid in the real world, which is why I have not included many in this book). To understand business, we need first to understand people.

Chapter 5

The Hierarchy of Needs

Why do people behave as they do? Various psychological schools, from Freud onwards, have advanced their own views on human motivation. One school of thinking which came to the fore in the 1950s, and which has been used to explain behaviour in both the workplace and the marketplace, is behaviouralism. I will not attempt to describe the whole field of behaviouralism here, but will instead focus on one of its chief underpinning concepts: the notion of need.

Our law of behaviouralism states that all human activity is driven ultimately by need. There are various kinds of needs, and they can be categorised in different ways. The oldest and still best known categorisation of needs is the 'hierarchy of needs' developed by the American psychologist Abraham Maslow. It has been argued that Maslow's ideas were influenced at least in part by Indian classical views on psychology and that the concepts of kama, artha, dharma and moksha all have counterparts in the hierarchy of needs.

Maslow argued that human needs can be classed into five categories:

1. **Physiological needs:** the needs for food, potable water, sleep, and so on, the things that are necessary to keep us alive.
2. **Safety needs:** the security of ourselves and our families and property from harm or damage.
3. **The need for 'belongingness' or love:** the need to be part of a social group and to have the esteem and respect of others.
4. **The need for self-esteem and self-respect.**
5. **The need for 'self-actualisation':** the need to be all that one can be, to fulfil one's destiny or to pursue a calling that one is born for.

Maslow believed that lower-order needs take precedence over higher-order needs. Physiological needs trump all others: if we do not have enough food, or enough sleep, we will set aside all other needs until those needs are satisfied. Maslow refers to this as the 'prepotency principle'. However, once we are assured of sufficient food and water, we will then turn to the next most important need, safety; and once we are safe and have shelter, we will then begin looking for social groups to which we can belong. Thus, as lower-order needs are satisfied we advance up the hierarchy, seeing the next level of need as most important.

Several points of clarification need to be made. First, it is possible to slip down the hierarchy as well as advance up it. People who are caught up in earthquakes or violent storms and lose their homes will slide down the hierarchy and seek to fulfill physiological and safety needs first and foremost. Second, not everyone enters the hierarchy at the bottom. Children born into middle-class backgrounds will start with their physiological and safety needs already fulfilled; indeed, if they go on to good jobs, they may never have to worry about these at all.

Self-actualisation the highest need of all, corresponds to some extent to the Indian concept of moksha. Maslow makes two points about self-actualisation. First, not everyone reaches this level, or wants to; most people are satisfied with achieving self-esteem. Second, full self-actualisation is not possible: it always remains a potential. Self-actualised people - mystics, artists, philosophers - continue to strive for something that remains out of reach. Maslow reasons that full self-actualisation would be akin to nirvana and would result in people ceasing to act at all, as they would no longer have any need to do so.

How does the hierarchy of needs work in the business context? Maslow's work has often been used to understand the motivation of employees. Why do people work? At the very bottom of the hierarchy they work to pay for food and shelter. Once these have been attained sooner in the case of our middle classes above, who already have safety and security - the driving need is for belongingness, to be an accepted part of a social group. We might use our earnings to consume goods and services which give us entrée into the social group we aspire to join: a house in a fashionable neighbourhood, a car that excites attention, good clothes, membership of a country club. For working-class people the needs might be more modest: a person might seek to earn enough money to allow them to enjoy a drink with their friends, or to be able to afford a kit so they can play cricket or other sports. Young people might seek to earn enough money to ask the object of their affections out on a date, to give gifts or to set up home together after marriage.

The other aspect of belongingness, and this is highly important, is that people make social groups at work, and find the comradeships of their fellow workers to be highly important. Many studies have shown that people seek the respect of their co-workers, and that their productivity and output improves when they feel part of a social group in the workplace. Some readers will have experienced this; I certainly have. A strong team with a good esprit de corps will perform well because its members are proud of themselves, of each other, and of the work that they do. At Titan, the Indian watchmaker, the staff refers to itself as 'Titanians' and is immensely proud of the company and its successes. This pride has continued even in times when labour relations at Titan were difficult. People might hate the management, one senior executive told me, but they still love the company.

Military units and sporting teams exhibit the same traits of belongingness and esprit de corps. That sense of teamwork and comradeship is vitally important, and good managers do all they can to foster this knowing that investment in such activity will pay their company back many times over.

Belongingness, though, is rarely enough. Most of us, especially as we grow older, seek something more. We want to know that what we do is right and good; we want to be able to look ourselves in the eye and know that the work we do matters to someone. Again, studies have shown that companies that provide this sense of meaning and purpose to work improve the self-esteem of employees. Their pride in themselves increases. They no longer come to work because they must in order to survive; they come to work because they want to do so. In the 1920s, researchers from Harvard University studying productivity at Western Electric's components plant near Hawthorne, Illinois, discovered that productivity among workers improved not because of any changes in the layout of the workplace or working conditions, but because they knew the researchers were studying them! The fact that they and their work was worth studying meant that workers developed higher self-esteem and a greater sense of self-worth. Again, most of us will have seen examples of this on a small scale. Think of how workers perk up and grow happier when a senior manager makes a walkabout and goes around to work stations talking to people. Even this little human contact improves self-esteem.

And then there is self-actualisation. Again, few people achieve this in the course of their work, and many do not even aspire to it. But some people do. And if their work allows them to become self-actualised, then these people can become the most powerful asset a company has. These are the designers, the innovators, the visionary strategists who see beyond the ordinary and explore the limits of the possible. They are what helps companies move forward faster than their competitors. They give their all, in part out of loyalty to the company, of course, but mostly because they feel compelled to, because something inside them is driving them. These people do not have to be senior executives; they might be ordinary workers. Spotting them and giving them the space they need to become self-actualised is not always easy, but again, the investment in doing so will be repaid many times over.

The hierarchy of needs can also be used to explain behaviour in the marketplace. People who do not have enough food or water will probably sacrifice other purchases until they have enough food and a supply of potable water; once that is achieved, they will seek to purchase shelter, either through rent or sale, and then to purchase goods that help them belong to a social group and so on. In her book *We Are Like That Only*, Rama Bijapurkar uses a version of the hierarchy of needs to segment the Indian consumer market:

1 **The resigned:** the very poorest people who are at subsistence level. Their only ambition is to survive; they have little hope of advancement.
2 **The strivers:** those people who were born into hardship but are prepared to work as long and hard as it takes in order to build a better life for themselves and their families.
3 **The mainstreamers:** those who have achieved at least a basic level of prosperity and are now seeking to consolidate their position. Their main goals are social acceptance and long-term security, although the need for self-esteem plays a role, too.
4 **The aspirers:** Bijapurkar calls these the 'wannabes', those who want the trappings of success and are motivated by the desire for status. One's own comfort matters, yes, but making the neighbours jealous is important too.
5 **The successful:** the aspirers who have made it to the top table. Achievement, recognition, and power are key motivating factors.

Similar segmentations can be developed for other countries and economies as well. The advantage over traditional sociographic segmentation methods such as ABC is that this segmentation identifies people's likely needs, regardless of their location or apparent status. What people think they need is what determines behaviour, not necessarily what they already have.

There are plenty of other ways of using the concept of need. Maslow's hierarchy has been criticised by later writers. One argument says that it is Western-centric and therefore does not explain behaviour in other cultures, but we have seen that it in fact works perfectly well in India, and I have argued that it applies in China too. A more serious complaint is that the hierarchy is apparently too rigid and does not reflect the fact that people can operate on several different levels. As a writer, I am at my most fulfilled when writing; this activity gives me a degree of self-actualisation. Away from my desk, I still seek meaning and self-esteem in other activities, and when not working I also seek belongingness. My position on the hierarchy changes depending on what I am doing and the time of day. And what about people who endure hardship and risk their lives in pursuit of a cause? Are the Syrian revolutionaries fighting against the Assad regime seeking to defend their homes and families, or are they self-actualised, ready to die in defence of what is right? It may be that they are both.

Maslow's simple concept has also been elaborated on by others. As noted, there are various forms of psychographic segmentation of markets based on behavioural models. In terms of workplace behaviour, two other American psychologists, Frederick Herzberg and Douglas McGregor, took Maslow's theories further. Herzberg added a list of environmental or 'hygiene' factors that also affect behaviour, including the quality of management in a firm, pay, working conditions, job security, and factors in one's personal life. McGregor developed the concept of Theory X and Theory Y. Theory X assumes that most people lack ambition; they will only work productively if they are coerced into doing so. Theory Y assumes that work is a natural human function, that most people will work effectively if motivated to do so and, what is more, most will naturally seek responsibility and try to rise to positions where they can exercise their own creativity and find more personal freedom. Theory X assumes people are motivated only by low-level physiological needs; Theory Y assumes that they are seeking self-esteem and self-actualisation.

Behaviouralism does not have all the answers when it comes to explaining human behaviour, but it does offer some absolute truths about responses to need. Employees work because they need to work and thus companies are able to produce goods and services. Customers buy goods and services because they need - or perceive that they need - those goods and services. Employees and customers are thus brought together in yin and yang fashion by the common factor of need. Can you think of how to use that common factor in a way that benefits employees, customers, and your company alike? Do so, and you will have come to terms with yet another paradox, and made it work in your favour.

Further Reading:

Bijapurkar, Rama (2008) *We Are Like That Only*, New Delhi: Penguin India.

Herzberg, Frederick (1966) *Work and the Nature of Man*, Cleveland: World Publishing Company.

Kaynak, Erdener and Kahle, Lynn R. (2000) *Cross-national Consumer Psychographics*, London: Routledge.

Maslow, Abraham (1954) *Motivation and Personality*, New York: Harper & Bros.

McGregor, Douglas (1960) *The Human Side of Enterprise*, New York: McGraw-Hill.

Chapter 6

Confucius's Golden Rule

This fundamental principle of ethics has several formulations, but the one we will use is, 'What one does not wish for oneself, one should not pass on to others; what one recognises as desirable for oneself, one should be willing to share with others' (Google's motto 'do no harm' is a simpler version of the same concept). Although I have taken this from Confucius, all the great religious and philosophical traditions have similar principles. Of course this principle is about more than just doing good; there are also sound practical reasons for following it. Self-interest as well as ethics dictates that we should follow this principle on the grounds that, as the Americans say, 'What goes around, comes around'.

Confucius, who lived from 551-479 BC, spent much of his life in pursuit of the ideal of a just and stable society which allows people to live together in peace and harmony. The creation of such a society, he believed, was an essential prerequisite to the creation of prosperity and wealth. He lived at a time when China's once-stable society was beginning to disintegrate and shortly after his death, China fell into the period known to historians as Zhanguo Shidai, or the Warring States era. Confucius saw the chaos coming and tried – in vain – to persuade rulers to adopt his recipe for stable government.

Confucius believed that stability in government and society was a balancing act. He argued the so-called 'Doctrine of the Mean', also sometimes known as the 'Great Similarity' or the 'Golden Mean' (similar concepts can be found in the Greek philosophy of Plato and Aristotle and in the works of the Indian writer Kautilya, of whom more in the next chapter): nothing should be done to excess. Equity and fairness depend, for example, on not too great a gap existing between the richest and the poorest. Confucius accepted that such a gap would always exist to some extent, but argued that too great a disparity would result in arrogance and high-handedness on the part of the rich, and resentment and anger on the part of the poor.

Above all, Confucius's Golden Mean relies on ethical behaviour. Some, such as the later Chinese writer Han Fei, criticised Confucius for apparently believing that people could be relied upon to behave ethically as part of the natural order of things, or that people had a natural instinct to be 'good'. Han Fei believed that people would only behave ethically if the law constrained them to do so, with rewards for those who did behave well and punishments for those who did not. But that is too simple a view of Confucius. Unlike Plato, who really did believe that human beings tend towards goodness and are naturally attracted to concepts such as beauty, truth, and justice, and unlike the authors of the Bhagavad Gita who equated ethical behaviour with duty to oneself, society, and God, Confucius recognised that self-interest played a role also. People would be more likely to behave ethically if they knew that others would behave in a similar manner to them; and similarly, that if they behaved unethically, others would behave unethically towards them.

My friend and colleague, the late Ian Rae, who owned and managed a business for several decades in China, often made exactly this point when talking about dealing with corruption. If you refuse to pay bribes to Chinese officials, he said, you will gain a reputation for probity and honesty which can be turned to your advantage. If however you do pay bribes, you will quickly get a reputation as a bribe-payer. More and more people will ask you for larger and larger bribes, the burden of expense thus increasing. What is more, honest people will regard you as a crook and will refuse to do business with you, meaning that you will be forced ever further into the company of the corrupt. Therefore, even if it is painful at times, the ethical way is the best.

Being ethical, then, can result in positive rewards. But does the reverse happen? Does unethical behaviour lead to negative impacts? Does what goes around really come around?

The answer is that very often it does. Sins committed in the past can come back to haunt the present, with a vengeance. Most readers will be familiar with the example of Enron, the energy trading company that was lauded as one of the great global success stories of the 1990s. But Enron's apparent success was built on a series of fabrications, false accounting, and deceits practiced on investors and staff alike. Those who were worried that something was wrong within the company were bullied into silence by strong-arm senior managers and corporate lawyers. External auditors who raised questions were told that they would lose valuable business with Enron unless they shut up. For quite a while, this worked. But in the end the deceits could be maintained no longer and the company collapsed.

Bernie Madoff, the now infamous American investment fund manager, took millions of dollars from clients to feed into his Ponzi-style investment scheme. Again, through deceit and false accounting, Madoff produced the illusion of success. His investors at first made healthy profits. But no Ponzi scheme can last indefinitely, as Stewart Weisman's inside look at the activities of the Bennett family in the 1990s makes clear. Madoff's house of cards ultimately collapsed.

Nick Leeson, the 'rogue trader' who ultimately brought down Baring's Bank, tried to cover losses on a trade by betting further large sums of the bank's money without telling his superiors. Each further loss was covered by a further bet, until the pressures finally led to the exposure of the truth. The bank collapsed and Leeson went to jail. Computer services company Satyam managed to cover up several years of false accounting and inflated returns until the failed takeover of Maytas led to a decline in the share price and once again the truth was exposed.

What happens? Why do these Ponzi schemes and rogue traders and false accountants get caught? Very often they are exposed whenever there is a downturn, either of the company's fortunes or in the wider economy, or both. Madoff, Satyam, and Enron all prospered during the economic boom; their unethical behaviour came to light when the economy faltered.

We know that economies will always go through cycles. Economies, as we saw earlier in this book, are subject to the laws of entropy and evolution: they grow and they decay. But companies and managers that behave unethically do not contribute to growth. False accounting is not growth; it is growth's mirror image. It is darkness, not light. False accountants and rogue traders increase the amount of entropy within an organisation, and the longer the situation goes on, the faster entropy increases. No unethical scheme, or society, or state, can last for long. Eventually, the past catches up. The forces of entropy become so strong that everything collapses. The only counterpart to entropy, as we saw earlier in this book, is evolutionary growth, genuine growth based on real value creation.

In the previous chapter we saw that the hierarchy of needs means that people behave according to the needs that drive them. How do we reconcile people's needs with ethical behaviour? A starving person might well commit crimes in order to get food. But the examples of unethical behaviour we have seen here were not committed by those desperate for food or safety. They were created by people whose driving need was ambition, self-esteem. Enron's top brass gloried in the adulation they received from the media during the years of prosperity. Nick Leeson of Barings confessed that he enjoyed his reputation as one of the most successful traders in Singapore, and feared the loss of that reputation if the truth were known. And yet, there was a hollowness. Those involved knew in their deepest hearts that what they were doing was wrong, that they did not deserve the respect they received.

Most unethical acts are committed by people who either do not know what the consequences of their actions will be, or believe that they can delay those negative consequences entirely. The first group are ignorant, and require education. The second are illogical. They need to be reminded that the law of 'what goes around comes around' is immutable. It may take years, even decades, for natural justice to work through, but it always will in the end. The law of entropy will not be denied.

Further Reading:

Arvedlund, Erin (2009) *Too Good to Be True: The Rise and Fall of Bernie Madoff*, New York: Penguin Portfolio.

Chen Huan-Chang (1911) *The Economic Principles of Confucius and His School*, New York: Longmans, Green; repr. Bristol: Thoemmes Press, 2002, with an introduction by Morgen Witzel.

Elkind, Peter and McLean, Bethany (2004) *The Smartest Guys in the Room: The Amazing Rise and Scandalous Fall of Enron*, New York: Penguin.

Lau, D.C. (1979) *Confucius: The Analects*, Harmondsworth: Penguin.

Weisman, Stewart L. (1999) *Need and Greed: The Story of the Largest Ponzi Scheme in American History*, Syracuse, NY: Syracuse University Press.

Chapter 7

Kautilya's Rule

The ancient Indian sage Kautilya, in his classic work on politics the *Arthashastra*, declared that: 'The king shall be ever active and discharge his duties; the root of wealth is activity, and evil its reverse'. This precept remains as true today as it was when it was written, around 2,300 years ago. Examining this precept tells us a number of things about the nature of work and output, and also about leadership.

Kautilya, also known as Chanakya, was born around 270 BC, probably near the town of Patna in the modern state of Bihar. He became the tutor and first minister of Chandragupta Maurya, the founder of the Mauryan empire. Like Confucius, Plato, and many other early writers on government and society, Kautilya was interested in establishing a set of precepts for government and management that would serve not only his own time but generations to come. He wrote down a series of precepts over the course of about 20 years, which were eventually collected under the title of *Arthashastra*. Many of the precepts are technical and concern managing functions such as the treasury and administration, and there are also sets of strategic principles that are reminiscent of those of the famous Chinese writer on strategy, Sunzi (Sun Tzu). Every so often, though, Kautilya pauses to consider the 'why' questions associated with administration and governance, not just the 'how' questions.

It is probable that Kautilya was aware of at least some of the ideas of Plato and Confucius. Traders coming over the Himalayan mountains from China might well have brought Confucian ideas with them (within a few years of Kautilya's death in 283 BC, Chandragupta's successor Ashoka would send Buddhist ideas back over the mountains into China). Plato's pupil Aristotle had been the tutor of Alexander the Great, and Chandragupta had been briefly allied with Alexander when the latter invaded in India and later conquered the short-lived Macedonian state in India and added it to his own empire. Kautilya would have had plenty of opportunities to get to know Platonist and Aristotelian ideas.

Kautilya believed that the primary duty of the king was to be the upholder of the dharma. In its most simple form, dharma means 'righteous duty', rather like the concept of natural law. The king's task is to make sure that this natural law is upheld and maintained, and that a balance is struck in society which enables all to co-exist peacefully. The royal bureaucracy exists to support and implement that policy. In practical terms, this means that the king should defend the state from attack, promote peace, order, justice and prosperity, and 'encourage moral, religious and material progress'.

The Golden Mean, as conceived of by Plato and Confucius, can appear to be a rather static concept, an unchanging equilibrium. Once a permanent harmony is achieved, the main task is to make sure that nothing disturbs that harmony; nothing and no one should step out of line to upset the balance. But Kautilya seems to have been aware of the law of entropy, although he does not call it by this name. He realised that dharma could not be maintained by striving to achieve a perfect state and then freezing everything in hopes that perfection would continue to last. The world around us is always shifting, and we must shift and evolve too. It is activity and work that, perhaps paradoxically, allow us to achieve the true natural order of things.

The purpose of the king and his bureaucrats, then, is not just to administer things as they were already ordered, but to help promote change and make it happen. Is it not much the same in modern business? Is not one of the primary responsibilities of a leader to be a change agent, to ensure that an organisation remains active and evolves and grows as it strives to reach its goals? Recall our earlier discussions in this book. There is no such thing as a steady state, only growth or decay. The organisations that survive are not necessarily the strongest or the most clever but those best suited to adapt, the most flexible.

The leader is responsible for ensuring that this flexibility exists. How he or she does so is encapsulated in Grove's Rule, which we will come to shortly (see Chapter 9). For the moment, it is enough to remember that this is what leaders do; it is what they are for. Leaders of businesses, like kings, are there to uphold the dharma, to make certain that the organisation is a place of growth, not entropy. Along with this, as Kautilya himself points out, one of their tasks is to root out the corruption that kills growth and increases entropy, and ensure that growth and change happen smoothly. Leaders are there to stimulate activity.

And, as Kautilya says, wealth comes from activity. No one gains wealth, no one creates value by doing nothing. Wealth, activity, and growth are all related to each other, just as lack of wealth, inactivity, and entropy are also related. The purpose of work is to create wealth, or as we might say today, create value. It is interesting to compare Kautilya's equation of activity = wealth with Confucius's equation that virtue = wealth; as he says in the *Daxue* (Great Learning), 'Virtue is the root, and wealth only the result.' So with the addition of this fourth element we can perhaps create a new equation: virtue + activity = growth, and virtue + activity + growth = wealth/value.

What are businesses for? Their purpose, too, is to uphold dharma, to contribute to the maintenance of the natural law. They do this by providing goods and services that people need, enabling them to climb the hierarchy of needs, to feed themselves and give them safety, belongingness and self-esteem and sometimes even self-actualisation. The inescapable conclusion is that businesses are there to serve society, not the other way around. That was the view taken by early Chinese and Indian scholars; that was the view taken by Islamic writers such as Abu Fadl al-Dimashqi in the eleventh century and Ibn Khaldun in the fourteenth century.

That was also the view taken by Jamsetji Nusserwanji Tata, the founder of the Tata group, when he stated that 'what comes from the people has gone back to the people'; i.e. that the wealth created through his business had been returned to the people who created it in the first place: his employees, their families and the people of India.

How many employers fully understand that their businesses are really only conduits through which wealth is created by the people who work for them? Come to that, how many workers do so? Over the past several centuries we have developed an adversarial system in most workplaces between management and workers, white-collar and blue-collar, each side thinking of the system as a contest between 'them' and 'us', each striving to gain advantage over the other. But this is not consistent with the need to uphold the dharma. Conflict between managers and workers is ultimately destructive, entropic. As R.N. Bose describes, Mahatma

Gandhi often reminded workers that they have a responsibility to the company and to the community; it is not just the company that is responsible for them. They, too, have a role to play in upholding the dharma.

Speculating on the reasons for poor relations between management and workers, the American engineer and consultant Harrington Emerson stumbled upon a paradox. Companies, he says, buy output from workers; they buy (by paying wages) the labour of workers which is necessary to make and sell goods. Workers, on the other hand, sell time, their own time which they provide to the company in exchange for wages. Workers are selling one thing, companies are buying another, which leads to confusion and misunderstanding as each fails to understand the value the other requires.

Kautilya's rule offers us a way of coming to terms with this paradox. Time and labour are both necessary for the creation of value. They are two halves of the same whole. Labour and time are co-dependent. The key is to achieve a balance between the needs of the worker and the needs of the organisation, and thus it flies in the face of reason for managers to push workers down and try to exploit them. As J.N. Tata said, it is the workers who create the wealth. Much more recently the Indian businessman Vineet Nayar argued against the concept of 'customer first'; instead, he said, companies ought to make employees their top priority. Motivated and trained employees will in turn put customers first and thus create value through their actions aimed at satisfying customers. In much the same way the Tata ethos, since the time of J.N. Tata, has been one of 'profit is a byproduct of what we do'.

And so we come back to the role of the leader, and the view espoused by Kautilya and echoed by Gandhi: the purpose of the leader is to uphold the dharma by making it possible for people to be active and thus create wealth. Gandhi's view of leadership was akin to the idea of 'servant leadership' developed in the 1970s, most notably by Robert Greenleaf in the book of that title. According to this view the leader is not the master of the organisation, but its servant. He or she is responsible for making sure that everyone else in the organisation works to their full potential and does all that they can do, and are all that they can be.

That, then, is the dharma of organisations: an internal harmony which allows everyone to work hard, contribute, and create.

This allows employees to satisfy their personal needs, not just through earning wages but right through to belongingness and self-esteem. By creating value for customers, they do something meaningful for society as a whole, and this helps them in turn to express and fully live their own humanity.

Further Reading:

Bose, R.N. (1956) *Gandhian Technique and Tradition in Industrial Relations*, Calcutta: All-India Institute of Social Welfare and Business Management.

Emerson, Harrington (1909) *Efficiency as a Basis for Operations and Wages*, New York: John R. Dunlap.

Greenleaf, Robert K. (1977) *Servant Leadership*, Mahwah, NJ: Paulist Press.

Kumar, Umesh (1990) *Kautilya's Thought on Public Administration*, New Delhi: National Book Organization.

Mason, Paul (2008) *Live Working or Die Fighting: How the Working Class Went Global*, London: Vintage.

Nayar, Vineet (2010) *Employees First, Customers Second: Turning Conventional Management Upside Down*, Boston: Harvard Business School Press.

Chapter 8

Buffett's Rule

The American investor Warren Buffett, the 'Sage of Omaha', has as one of his maxims the following rule: 'Never invest in something you don't understand'. During the 'dotcom' era, the high-technology boom that turned into a bubble, Buffett and his Berkshire Hathaway group resolutely refused to be drawn into investing in risky technology shares. The share price of Berkshire Hathaway itself declined as a result, while investors chasing the lure of higher profits in technology shares distanced themselves from the company. When the bubble burst in 2001 Buffett's strategy was vindicated – Berkshire Hathaway weathered the crisis intact.

Now in his eighties, Buffett once worked as an investment salesman and a stockbroker before founding his own investment group. His knowledge of financial markets and their workings is based largely on personal experience. He has been highly critical of financial modelling and other techniques which promise certain returns, claiming that 'it is better to be 90 per cent right than 100 per cent wrong'.

Let us look first at the rule itself: never invest in something you don't understand. It sounds like common sense. Most investors, most of the time, will sit down and analyse certain standard things about an investment before making it. What is the potential return on that investment? What are the associated risk factors? When deciding whether to invest in a company we might look at its financial performance, its track record in areas such as innovation, the performance and character of its directors, the stated strategy of the business, and so on. We would aim to know quite a lot about the business before we invested in it.

But Buffett is not just talking about knowledge. He is talking about understanding. It is quite possible to amass a great deal of knowledge while still having very little understanding. We all know how to operate a computer. But how many of us understand what goes on inside it? We all look at weather forecasts – here in Britain more often than in other parts of the world, perhaps – but how many of us really understand the forces of the weather and climate? Do we know how things work, and even more importantly, why they work as they do?

Many readers will remember the dotcom bubble when a whole generation of high-technology companies sprang up with a view to taking advantage of the seemingly limitless promise of the Internet. Quite a few of these companies floated themselves on the stock market in order to raise capital for their expensive software development projects. Investors gathered knowledge about these companies. They looked at the promised returns on investment, at the characters of the companies themselves, and the track records of the people who founded them. Many of these people had fine pedigrees as entrepreneurs, engineers, and so on. There was an element of risk, but the rewards appeared to outweigh the risks.

But most of these investors had no real idea of what they were buying. They looked at the promised returns, but they did not take the necessary next step and ask how the money to pay those returns was going to be generated. Was there any proof that customers would migrate to this new model of doing business as quickly as the entrepreneurs hoped they would? There was none. Instead, seduced by the promise of high returns, investors made decisions based on faith, not understanding. Many failed to get their money back. In the end, the transition to Internet business proved to be an evolution, not a revolution. It took many years for amazon.com to post its first profits. The great majority of these dotcom ventures failed completely, taking the investors' money down the drain with them.

Buffett and others like him balked at making these investments because they did not understand them. Buffett was not predicting disaster in the late 1990s when he made his famous statement; for all he knew, the other investors might well have been right and there was a fortune to be made. But he was not prepared to invest based on faith alone. He said, in effect, 'I do not understand this business model, and because I do not understand it, it is not for me'. He walked away and in the process endured criticism from other investors and commentators. But he was proved right.

Think of an example closer to the present: the trade in derivatives, especially in the housing market which sprang up in the decade before the present one. As Pablo Triana describes in his book *Lecturing Birds on Flying*, the market in these derivatives was based on complex mathematical models understood by only a few. The rest of the market trusted the models and made investments based on faith. When the market in these derivatives collapsed – according to Triana, at least in part because of flaws in the models themselves – those companies which had invested heavily in financial products that they did not understand suffered heavily; Lehman Brothers collapsed and many other banks required bailouts or were taken over. Others such as HSBC and Santander which had been suspicious about this bubble from the start were less exposed and came through the crisis more or less undamaged; Santander was even able to take over some of its stricken rivals. Yet banks continue to invest in things they do not understand. In 2012, J.P. Morgan became the latest to suffer the consequences of violating Buffett's rule; it will not be the last.

This is not to say that if we do not invest in things we do not understand we will always come out on top. There is a chance that our lack of understanding is based on ignorance of the true situation, and that others with better understanding and insight will make money while we are left behind. It is just the kind of uncertainty and insecurity which leads people who do not understand a phenomenon to join the rush towards it anyway. This is the famous herd instinct, discussed by Robert Shiller in *Irrational Exuberance*, and earlier as a more general social phenomenon by Charles Mackay in his book *Extraordinary Popular Delusions and the Madness of Crowds*. Shiller and Mackay both point out that human behaviour during economic booms and bubbles is irrational, and Buffett agrees; in 2010 he described economic bubbles as 'self-delusionary'. But the delusions and the herd instinct are based on uncertainty and insecurity. The rush to buy shares in technology or in housing derivatives was motivated at least in part by the needs for belongingness and self-esteem. Here is how a colleague described to me the mood on Wall Street in 2005-06 at the height of the bubble: 'Everyone said, "There's a game on! You've got to get in the game!"' In other words, 'place your bets, ladies and gentlemen, even if you do not know what you are betting on.'

The answer to uncertainty and insecurity is knowledge and understanding. If you are going to be an investor you have to not only know the market in which you are investing, you also have to understand it. Knowing the parameters, understanding price movements and the like tells you how the market works, but you also have to dig deeper and ask the all-important 'why' questions. Why does the market act in this way? What drives behaviour and attitudes? If someone promises a high return, where is the money going to come from that will pay those returns? What is the ultimate source of value creation in this market?

At its heart, Buffett's Rule reminds us of the law of unintended consequences (see Chapter 4) and asks us to consider what the consequences of an investment decision might be. If we do not understand those consequences, we should take one of two options: study the situation more thoroughly in order to gain better understanding, or walk away from the investment. The third option, proceeding without understanding, is always the worst.

This applies across the board, not just to investments in financial markets but to the other kinds of investments that companies make all the time, and have to make if they are to grow and prosper. Here are some examples:

Investments in other countries. We would never think of making an investment in another country without first researching that country's business environment and culture, right? Yet, shockingly, many companies do exactly that. Western companies investing in East Asia have been burned over and over again by their lack of understanding of different attitudes to issues such as contracts. The American bicycle maker Schwinn was the largest bicycle brand in the world until it decided to outsource design and production to partner companies in Taiwan. Schwinn did not check its contracts carefully enough, and the Taiwanese partners were able to take over much of Schwinn's markets. Within a few years they were the largest bicycle makers in the world and Schwinn was seeking protection from bankruptcy. The same mistakes are made in other parts of the world too. Dutch supermarket chain Royal Ahold was a huge success in its home market, but failed to understand the complex and highly competitive American market before investing heavily there. Losses on this investment brought about the collapse of the entire company.

Investments in people. We spend immense amounts of money on recruiting people. We use sophisticated psychographic and personality profiling tools to make sure we get the right people for the right job. We hire them, and then we forget about them. We expect that they will deliver loyally as we ask and forget that they have needs too. Perplexed by this, the American engineer Harrington Emerson noted that a railway company might spend $10,000 a year maintaining and servicing a locomotive (he was writing in 1908) to keep it in tip-top condition, but would balk at spending $10 on something which might improve the lives and working conditions of employees. A hundred years on and in most companies, nothing has changed. Smart companies follow Vineet Nayar's dictum and invest in employees because they know that happy employees create happy customers. Most companies still do not understand this and much of the initial investment they make in recruiting people is wasted.

Investing in mergers and acquisitions. Numerous research studies over the past 20 years have shown that the majority of M&As – between 65 and 80 per cent, depending on the study – fail to deliver the expected result. Some fail disastrously, such as the famous merger of Time Warner and AOL, which resulted in a breathtaking loss of $100 billion in the first year after the merger. The majority of M&As fail because of a lack of understanding. The prospective partners know the facts about each other: turnover, profit, costs, productivity, and so on. But they do not understand each other. Their cultures simply are not compatible. This was the basic underlying problem at Time Warner/AOL. It was the basic problem, too, during the disastrous merger between German car maker Daimler and America's Chrysler, agreed in 1998. It was not just language that separated the two but fundamental personal and corporate values and ideas about how businesses should be run. Eventually the entire merger began to collapse as the forces of entropy took over, and an expensive demerger had to be put into place a few years later.

Investing in technology. While e-commerce was the most visible face of the dotcom boom of the late 1990s, other companies were caught up in the bubble too. Companies invested millions in IT capacity in the late 1990s on the assumption that the costs would be recouped by operating efficiencies. Few investing companies knew what they were investing in. I recall seeing a research report around the time, based on interviews with CEOs, in which nearly all confessed they did not have a clue what this new technology was all about. 'The only thing that keeps me awake at night,' remarked one, 'is not knowing what my chief information officer is doing'. By 2002/03 it had become clear that most companies had not achieved enough operating efficiencies to pay back the initial investment, and most never would.

Investing in products. It would seem to be common sense to make and sell products, only if it is clear that customers want to buy them. Again, a shockingly large number of companies invest in new products without understanding the market they are in. In the late 1970s the British car maker Austin Rover, trying to turn around its declining fortunes, embarked on a strategy which it labelled 'production-led recovery'. Austin Rover would rebuild its financial health by producing fewer but better cars, turning out three new high-quality models which would rebuild its brand image among customers. The firm's executives assumed that customers would flock to buy their cars, but they failed to understand the nature of either the domestic or the export market. Customers had moved on to other brands, and Austin Rover's new cars did not catch on. Further, by reducing production volumes, Austin Rover fell foul of decreasing economies of scale and its unpopular cars were also expensive. 'Production-led recovery' turned out to be a myth and the company's market share and fortunes began to decline.

'Never invest in what you don't understand' is a rule to be followed in all of business, not just when investing in financial markets. It is not enough to know how things happen; always and continuously, we must ask *why* they happen.

Further Reading:

Buffett, Warren and Cunningham, Lawrence A. (2008) *The Essays of Warren Buffett*, New York: John Wiley & Sons.

Mackay, Charles (1995) *Extraordinary Popular Delusions and the Madness of Crowds*, London: Wordsworth.

Shiller, Robert J. (2005) *Irrational Exuberance*, Princeton: Princeton University Press.

Triana, Pablo (2009) *Lecturing Birds on Flying: Can Mathematical Theories Destroy the Financial Markets?* Chichester: John Wiley.

Chapter 9

Grove's Rule

Andrew Grove, CEO and later chairman of Intel, famously declared that in business 'only the paranoid survive'. If you think that something out there in the business world is waiting to attack you and your firm, that is because it probably is. Grove argued that no one can foresee change and that the most violent and catastrophic changes are also the most unpredictable. Understanding and accepting Grove's Rule encourages firms to develop the robustness and mental toughness that are required to survive in times of turmoil.

Grove himself is no stranger to turmoil. Born in Hungary, he grew up during the Second World War and then the communist period, escaping the country after the failed revolution of 1956. In New York he held a number of jobs including working as a waiter in a diner while going to university. After taking a PhD in engineering he joined Fairchild Semiconductor where he worked with two legendary figures of the early computer industry, Robert Noyce and Gordon Moore (about whom see Chapter 10). When Noyce and Moore left Fairchild to found microchip maker Intel in 1968, Grove went with them. He became CEO of Intel in 1987, going on to become chairman. Today he is revered by many; the late Steve Jobs of Apple once said that he 'idolised' Grove, and *Time* magazine named Grove its 'Man of the Year' in 1997.

For Grove, management is about performance. He is less interested in what managers do than in what they produce. In one of his early books, *High Output Management*, he drew on his experiences as a waiter in a diner to describe the art of managers as similar to the cooking and serving of breakfast. All the ingredients have to be right, everything has to be delivered at the right time and place, but the fundamental purpose of all of this activity is to satisfy the customer eating the meal. Similarly, the fundamental purpose of management is to create output that satisfies customers. At Intel, the managerial output is silicon chips; the output of surgeons are healed patients, and so on. Managers also need to know what motivates their employees, and in his writings Grove refers specifically to Maslow's hierarchy of needs (see Chapter 5) and reminds managers that they must be aware of how needs motivate employees.

Grove was aware of the principles behind Darwin's Rule (see Chapter 2) and the forces of change and growth. As CEO of Intel, he regarded it as his job to ensure that the company never stood still and was constantly moving, progressing and advancing. As leader of the company he was responsible for its strategy, and he understood very well the uncertainties and problems that surround the implementation of any strategy. In the nineteenth century the famous writer on strategy Karl von Clausewitz had developed the notion of 'friction', the building up of unforeseen events and situations that conspires to slow down or even completely halt strategies in their tracks. It only needs a few little events – a key manager goes off on sick leave, a particular process costs more and takes longer than expected, vital components from a supplier do not arrive on time – and the original strategic plan is knocked back.

A disciple of Clausewitz, the Prussian field marshal Helmuth von Moltke, remarked that 'no plan survives contact with the enemy'. In business today we can simply say, 'no plan survives'. I tell my MBA students that if ever they sit down and make a plan and then execute that plan exactly as originally planned with no changes, no delays, and on budget, they should mark that day on the calendar and open a bottle of champagne – because it will probably never happen again.

Clausewitz perceived friction as being an entropic force, starting off with small changes but then increasing at an ever-accelerating rate. Grove has a different view. Instead of seeing change and decay as continuous forces, he believes there are periods of calm interrupted by big, unplanned, and unanticipated disruptions, which he terms 'strategic inflection points'. The appearance of one these points can mean new opportunities, or it can mean the beginning of the end, depending on how the business responds. Formal planning cannot anticipate these kinds of changes, and therefore managers have to be able to respond to the unanticipated. The advent of the personal computer was an obvious example of a strategic inflection point, forcing companies such as IBM and DEC to adapt or go out of business. The development of digital photography which pushed Kodak into the wall is another.

This is where organisational 'paranoia' comes in. In his book *Only the Paranoid Survive*, Grove uses the word 'paranoia' in a rather playful sense; he is not referring to mental illness, but to the idea that businesses always need to be on their guard, watching out for rivals and scanning the environment for potential threats. 'Only the paranoid survive' relates closely to Darwin's view that 'it is not the strongest that survive, nor the most intelligent, but those that are best capable of adaptation'. Grove also takes both Darwin's original view that competition is a key force determining adaptations and evolution, and the corresponding view of Alfred Russel Wallace that environmental forces also play a role in shaping evolution. Grove sees both as equally powerful. As CEO of Intel he encouraged his staff to think up scenarios and have discussions about how the company would solve a particular problem if it arose, no matter how unlikely the circumstances. To Grove, no problem was too unlikely. His doctrine was that 'what can happen, probably will happen'.

Grove's approach to strategic thinking was to encourage flexibility and adaptability and not be too wedded to plans which might have to be altered or even jettisoned at a moment's notice. His approach fits into the 'thinking' or 'emergent' approach to strategy, which contrasts with the formal, planned approach which evolved in American business thinking in the 1950s and 1960s. The thinking approach goes back at least to the fifth century BC; Chinese general Sunzi (Sun Tzu) wrote in *The Art of War* that the prerequisites to success are: knowledge of one's own capabilities, knowledge of the enemy's capabilities and intentions (competition), and knowledge of the terrain on which the contest will take place (environment). Sunzi did not advise formal plans; instead, he encouraged commanders to gather knowledge and then act wisely as the circumstances dictate. Much more recently the Spanish writer on strategy Jorge Vasconcellos e Sá stated that there are four essentials to success: knowledge of the opposition, knowledge of the environment or terrain, a clear focus on the desired goal, and surprise – or at least, the ability not to be surprised by unforeseen events. Grove's 'paranoid' organisation has all four of these qualities.

Like Japanese strategy guru Kenichi Ohmae, Grove believes in the power of continuously thinking about problems and wrestling with them, not so much in order to solve the problem but to achieve a high state of mental alertness and readiness. Ohmae compared the mind of the strategist to a muscle: the more you exercise it, the stronger it will grow. People who think about strategic problems all the time, as both Ohmae and Grove advise, will be better prepared for a crisis when it comes and not simply stand like deer trapped in the headlights, in Ohmae's famous metaphor, panicking and not knowing what to do next.

The paranoid organisation, Grove says, never takes anything for granted. Managers need to engage in constant debate, sharing information and generating new ideas. Always challenge the data, Grove says, ask what it is really telling you. As we saw with Buffett's Rule, the need is for understanding as well as knowledge.

Grove's own company, Intel, shows the value of organisational paranoia very powerfully. In 1994 a fault in the company's Pentium FDIV microprocessor was discovered only after the chips had been installed in many thousands of computers. This was a strategic inflection point, an event that could have wrecked the company's reputation. So great was the shock that it took a short time for Intel to respond. When it did, however, the response was swift and decisive. Amid a blaze of publicity, Intel offered to replace all the defective chips – immediately and free of charge. This operation cost the company more than half a billion dollars, but it saved Intel's reputation and brand.

Fast actions and quick reactions are essential. In 2000, Air France responded quickly to the crash of one of its Concorde supersonic airliners, grounding the entire fleet and announcing an immediate inquiry. The airline's share price dipped briefly but quickly recovered. Around the same time, a series of accidents involving Ford cars fitted with Firestone tyres was linked to tyre failures. Firestone first tried to ignore the incident, and even after admitting the problem its response was hesitant and slow. People lost confidence in Firestone and Ford, whose partnership with Firestone went right back to the foundation of both companies, ended its supplier relationship with the company. Sinking towards oblivion, Firestone was bought out by its Japanese rival Bridgestone.

The paranoid survive because they are able to adapt to change and do not surrender to the forces of entropy. The complacent perish because they cannot change and allow entropy to overwhelm them. Managers must remember this, and adapt their own thinking and behaviour accordingly.

Further Reading:

Clausewitz, Karl von (1819) *Vom Kriege*, ed. and trans. Michael Howard and Peter Paret, *On War*, Princeton: Princeton University Press, 1984.
Grove, Andrew (1983) *High Output Management*, New York: Random House.
Grove, Andrew (1996) *Only the Paranoid Survive: How to Exploit the Crisis Points that Challenge Every Company and Career*, New York: HarperCollins.
Mintzberg, Henry and Quinn, James Brian (eds) (1988) *The Strategy Process*, Englewood Cliffs, NJ: Prentice Hall.
Ohmae, Kenichi (1982) *The Mind of the Strategist*, New York: McGraw-Hill.
Sunzi (1963) *The Art of War*, trans. L. Giles, ed. Samuel B. Griffiths, Oxford: Oxford University Press.
Vasconcellos e Sá, Jorge (2005) *Strategy Moves*, London: Pearson Education.

Part 3

The Laws of Organisation

The third part of this book deals with principles of organisation. Whereas the previous parts dealt with the mindsets of individuals, here we look at the dynamics of groups and the problems these pose for management.

The dynamics of organisation have been widely studied and commented on, and this book is by no means a complete discussion of the subject. What I have tried to do here is isolate certain fundamental principles that can always be observed, as omnipresent as entropy or evolution. Of the 11 'laws' in this section, 10 are principles that need to be respected and followed. The principle observed in Chapter 15, however, should *not* be followed and indeed should be avoided at all costs!

I was not certain at first of where to include Moore's Law concerning the growth of computing capacity, but finally decided to place it as the first chapter in this section on the grounds that (1) a discussion of Gordon Moore follows logically after a discussion of Andrew Grove, and (2) Moore's Law has a profound impact on organisations, not least in the amount of entropy that is produced as a result.

Productivity is also the theme of our eleventh law, the Pareto Principle or 80/20 rule. Paradoxically, computers are increasing in productive power but it seems that this benefits some of us more than others. Understanding the true sources of productivity and value creation within an organisation is vital to knowing how the organisation works and how power is distributed through it.

The rule of the span of control also concerns power and how it is used and exercised. The ability of any one individual, or even a team, to control and govern an organisation is limited by the span of control, and this has many implications for the ways in which organisations are governed. Parkinson's Law, likewise, shows what happens when entropy begins to take over and power and control begin to erode, while Roberto Michels' concept of the 'iron law of oligarchy' shows how power is always concentrated in the hands of a few. But are the few fit to wield power? The Peter Principle shows that people are promoted into positions of power in spite of their unfitness for power – or perhaps even because of it. Entropy, it seems, can be a force propelling people to the top of organisations.

Entropy's effect on the world of finance was noticed centuries ago. Gresham's Law, on the effect that bad money drives out good money, is as true today as it ever was, and like Buffett's Rule, it has applicability right across the world of business, not just in financial markets.

Our final four 'laws' are precepts that can hopefully help to guide managers through the difficult jungle of modern organisations and through the clashing forces of entropy and growth and paradox. Martin's rules, formulated by the great seventeenth-century banker, relate back to Buffett's Rule and offer guidance to the perplexed in terms of investment and money management.

Fayol's 14 points are time-honoured principles for the management of an organisation in terms of power and control. Deming's 14 points bring Fayol up to date and add dimensions concerning quality and freedom. Finally Drucker's Rule, that the purpose of business is the creation of customers, is a principle that no business large or small can afford to ignore – at least not for very long.

Chapter 10

Moore's Law

The physicist Gordon Moore, one of the founders of Fairchild Semiconductor and of Intel, stated that the transistor density of integrated circuits doubles every 24 months. In other words, computers double in processing power every two years (the figure is sometimes given as every 18 months, but this is Moore's original statement). As computers are part of the fabric of most modern technology, this has implications for how we approach innovation and new technology.

Understanding Moore's Law is crucial to knowing how and when - and when not - to invest in new computer technology. In Chapter 8, Buffett's Rule, we discussed the importance of not investing in something that we do not understand. But how can we hope to understand something that doubles in complexity every two years? The home computers that I began to use in the 1980s resemble the laptop on which I am writing this book about as much as a Stone Age flint axe resembles a chainsaw. It is not just that the technology itself has become much more complex; what that technology can do, how it affects our work and our lives, has increased in complexity too.

Moore's successor as CEO of Intel, Andrew Grove, wrote in his book *Only the Paranoid Survive* that technology has become an unstoppable force. What technology can do, he said, it will do. The scientists and inventors who are responsible for new technology are constantly probing the boundaries of the possible. Some detect a slight slowing of the rate of technological progress - it has been argued that by the end of this decade the doubling of capacity will take place every three years, not every two - and eventually of course the physical boundaries of the possible will be reached. But that day seems a long way off.

With complexity, as we saw in Chapter 1, comes entropy. The more complex an organisation becomes, the greater the amount of entropy that is present within the system. Greater complexity means that more things can potentially go wrong. And yet we invest in technology in the hope that it will make things simpler, easier, and more efficient. We have found another paradox: the paradox of technology. The more effective a piece of technology is at doing the job for which it was designed, the more complex that piece of technology is likely to be.

This effect was first noticed by another physicist, Norbert Wiener, while working on anti-aircraft fire control systems for the US navy during the Second World War (this was, of course, in the days before computers). Wiener designed feedback and control systems that would identify targets attacking a ship from several directions at once and ensure that the maximum number of guns engaged each target. He observed that a system which did this effectively was necessarily a more complex system, because in order to be flexible and reactive the system needed many more moving parts which needed to work together. A later scholar, Jay Wright Forrester at the Massachusetts Institute of Technology, used Wiener's ideas to create what he called 'industrial dynamics', a theory of understanding how the parts of organisations work together in complex form.

To observe Wiener's principle in action, pick up a cat, hold it upside down a few feet above the ground and then let go. The cat will twist itself in mid-air and land on its feet. Do the same to a human being, and he or she will land on her back or her side. Cats are more flexible than people because their spinal columns are more complex: they have more vertebrae and more muscles than we do, and these extra 'parts' enable them to move more quickly.

The next time you get into a car to drive somewhere, consider how complex a machine it is. Early automobiles were built simply with perhaps only a few dozen individual parts. They were also slow, low-powered, difficult to steer, and prone to breaking down. Modern cars have thousands of components, and these have been enhanced by computer technology. Former US president Bill Clinton once commented that the average Ford car had more computer technology than any of the Apollo moon missions of the 1960s. And Clinton said that more than 10 years ago, so according to Moore's Law cars now have five times as much computer technology as they did then.

As Forrester observed, it is the same with business organisations. Businesses today are more complex than they were 10 years ago, and we can infer that the larger the business, the faster the rate of increase in complexity over that time. And according to the paradox we observed above, much of that complexity has been created by the introduction of new technology. From robotic manufacturing and CAD-CAM on the shop floor to complex financial models in the finance department, from e-commerce and computer relationship management (CRM) software in the marketing department to automated payroll systems and accounting programs and, of course, the ubiquity of e-mail and mobile phones and the increasing prominence of social media, technology has had a huge impact. One consequence, indeed, has been that in many industries such as consulting and banking, there is no longer such a thing as a day off, or even a night off. People have their BlackBerries or smartphones switched on at all times and even keep them beside their beds when they sleep. Working hours, as Charles Handy pointed out, have become longer and work has become more complex.

And yet, this complexity has had a positive impact. Cars today are safer and more fuel efficient than ever before. Businesses, and people, are more productive than ever before too. Studies show global productivity rising at an ever-increasing rate, and even the deep global economic slowdown that began in 2008 has not had a significant impact on global productivity per person.

In order to understand how to deal with Moore's Law, we need to refer back to the paradox of entropy and growth. The doubling of technological capacity that Moore observed creates complexity, which in turn creates entropy; but that complexity also leads to flexibility and adaptability, which is necessary for growth. So, as investors in technology, our purpose must be to invest in those specific technologies that maximise flexibility while minimising the entropic effect.

By this point you are probably saying to yourself, 'What on earth is he talking about?' Let me put it another way. The aim is not 'to invest in technology'– no one should invest in technology just for its own sake. The aim is to invest in the 'right' technology that will benefit the organisation. And how do we decide what is the 'right' technology? The answer must be this: the 'right' technology is technology that is fit for the purpose, that will enhance the company's ability to serve customers and meet its goals now and in the immediate future. That is the most important yardstick of all.

And that measure will also differ from company to company. Managers need to do periodic reviews of technological capacity and requirements, during which they should ask four questions:

1 Is our current technology suite performing in line with our current and likely future needs?
2 Is there other technology available which would enable us to improve performance, or is such technology likely to emerge in the near future?
3 Are the advantages of adopting a new technology sufficient to outweigh the disadvantages (cost of installation, training, and recruitment of skilled employees, etc.)?
4 How long will it be before industry standards change and our existing technology becomes obsolete?

Answering the first three is quite easy, and can be done using existing metrics and data. Answering the fourth is the hardest. Many people take Moore's Law to mean that they must update every two years, and make investments accordingly. I know of people who, without fail, trade in their old car and upgrade to a new one every two years. Their argument for doing so is that they must have the latest model. Even though the old car is still perfectly serviceable and driveable, newer cars will have additional important features, such as satellite navigation, or offer greater fuel economy. What these drivers do not do is sit down and calculate whether they will earn back the cost of this investment every two years. Even given the reduced fuel costs that accrue from improved fuel economy, given the short time horizon of the investment, very few of them do.

As we saw in Chapter 8, in the late 1990s companies around the world invested hundreds of millions in new communications technology. Few understood what they were really buying and most did not see a positive return on investment. Around the same time, telecommunications companies in Britain invested further hundreds of millions in replacing old-style copper wire telephone cables with fibre-optic cables intended to handle the new generation of communication technologies. Then came broadband, and with it the discovery that fibre-optic cables are not particularly suited to handling broadband, thus necessitating still more investment in cabling.

China and India offer a different perspective on the problem. Instead of making massive nationwide investments in fibre-optic cabling, the planners there looked out at the longer horizon and saw the next big thing: mobile telephony. They waited, and then invested heavily in mobile technology. Hundreds of millions of people in both countries have mobile phones but do not have, and have never had, landlines. They have no need for them.

So, how do we deal with Moore's Law? Not by slavish adherence, not by religious investing in new technology every two years to keep up with the cycle. Moore's Law is more profound than that. It suggests that technology will continue to change for the foreseeable future, and even offers us a framework for anticipating change. With 3G mobile phones now standard, we know that 4G is on the way. What might it offer, what might it do? We cannot predict for certain, but if we have enough organisational 'paranoia' we can begin to think of possibilities and plan how we will react. What are the other big 'inflection points' in technology that are coming up? Should we invest at this point in Moore's cycle? Or should we take the chance that our present technology is 'good enough', fit for purpose, and wait for the next cyclical change, the next doubling, and invest then? Will the money we save now by waiting outweigh the costs of future investment? Or will investment now result in quick efficiency savings?

These are the kinds of questions that need to be asked and answered. It is easy to know about technology, easy to understand its parameters and performance values and its technical capacity. It is harder to understand what that technology can do for the organisation. To make that final step, there is one further element that needs to be considered if we are to deal with the paradox of technology.

The economist Paul Strassman, in his book *The Business Value of Computers*, made the point that computers, like all technologies, are effectively artifacts. The business value of a computer, he said, is what it will fetch at auction, nothing more. We may invest $10 million in a computer system, but the value of that system itself is only what we will get if you try to sell it on. And as anyone who has tried to sell used computers knows, that value is often precisely zero, especially if the computer or system is more than a year or two old.

What gives computers, and all technology, their value is what happens when you put them in the hands of people. A Stone Age flint axe is just a lump of stone, until a skilled hunter picks it up and begins to use it. A computer sits silently, a box of plastic and wires and silicon, until someone programmes it and gives it commands – and makes it come to life. Human agency and human intellect are what gives technology its value. And so, if we invest $10 million in a new computer system but our staff do not have the skills and knowledge to work it effectively, that investment is largely wasted. Again, one might think this is common sense; investing in new technology must be accompanied by training so that people know how to use it well. In practice, training is often sketchy and simplistic. One colleague who has done research in this field reckons that most people in most offices use about 10 per cent of the actual capacity of the computers installed there.

The final lesson that comes from examining Moore's Law is this: if the power of computers is doubling every two years, or three, it follows that the skill levels and knowledge required of the people who use those computers must increase, also. Each investment in technology must be accompanied by a corresponding investment in people. If this is done, then growth will result. But if there is a disparity, if the skills of the people fall behind while the technology advances, then entropy will begin to increase. Costs and complexities will spiral upwards until, in the end, the entire organisation is threatened. Managing the paradox of technology requires that technology and people should develop together.

Further Reading:

Brock, David C. (2006) *Understanding Moore's Law: Four Decades of Innovation*, Philadelphia: Chemical Heritage Foundation.

Forrester, Jay Wright (1961) *Industrial Dynamics*, Portland, OR: Productivity Press.

Grove, Andrew (1996) *Only the Paranoid Survive: How to Exploit the Crisis Points that Challenge Every Company and Career*, New York: HarperCollins.

Strassman, W. Paul (1990) *The Business Value of Computers*, New Canaan, CT: Information Economics Press.

Chapter 11

The Pareto Principle

Also known as the 80/20 rule, the Pareto Principle was formulated by the American engineer and quality management guru Joseph Juran. When researching problems in production systems, Juran found that approximately 80 per cent of quality defects were created within about 20 per cent of the production process. In other words, most of each production system actually operates quite well, and only small parts of it create problems. This principle helped Juran and his colleagues to zero in more quickly on those elements of the process where remedial work was needed – and also to know which parts were working well already and did not need fixing. The principle is still well known to those who work in quality management, and Pareto charts are often used to identify the sources of defects.

There has been some confusion around the name. Juran called this principle the 'Pareto Principle' in honour of the late nineteenth and early twentieth century Italian economist and sociologist Vilifredo Pareto, who had observed in passing that 80 per cent of the wealth in Italy was concentrated in the hands of 20 per cent of the population. It was thought at first that Pareto had invented the Pareto Principle and Juran had to clarify matters and point out that he himself was responsible for the name. The Pareto Principle also should not be confused with Pareto optimality, an economic concept that Pareto did discuss at some length. It is also important to note that the 80/20 rule is not a mathematical principle, and very seldom do the proportions work out to exactly 80 per cent and 20 per cent. The Pareto Principle is more a rule of thumb – but it is a surprisingly durable and valid one, with applications in many spheres of human activity. Here are a few examples:

- Economic surveys have shown that around 80 per cent of the world's wealth is controlled by 20 per cent of its population (thus confirming Pareto's original observation).
- Studies in America have shown that 20 per cent of hazards are responsible for 80 per cent of accidents in the workplace.

- In business, 80 per cent of profits are generated by 20 per cent of customers; similarly, 80 per cent of complaints are generated by 20 per cent of customers (not usually the same ones).
- Volume retailers often find 20 per cent of the product line generates 80 per cent of sales.
- 80 per cent of the value that businesses create comes from the efforts of 20 per cent of employees.

Again, these are rules of thumb. The actual percentages vary and the precise number does not really matter. The main point is that in many fields, the bulk of activity derives from a relatively small number of sources. Take for example the rule that 80 per cent of profits are generated by 20 per cent of customers. This means that 80 per cent of businesses customers are occasional or one-off purchasers who add little to the company's profits – or may even be causing the company to generate losses. One American accounting firm found exactly that serving many of its small business clients was actually costing the company more than the revenue these accounts generated.

How should we react to the Pareto Principle? In marketing, it is generally accepted that businesses should concentrate their efforts on building relationships with the important 20 per cent, and that would seem to be common sense. It is tempting to think that if we devote more attention to the 80 per cent we can convert them into regular customers, but there may be many reasons why this is not possible. It is, however, important to understand why that 80 per cent do not come back to shop more often or at all.

It has been suggested that businesses should 'fire' those customers in the 80 per cent bracket as it is clearly less profitable to serve them. That is risky. For one thing, telling people you no longer want their custom is an excellent way to annoy them, thus generating bad publicity and negative word of mouth (and social networking means the chance of this happening has gone up dramatically). Also, casual customers sometimes convert into more regular customers, even after long periods of time, if their initial reactions to the company and its products and services are favourable. Their own economic circumstances and needs might change, or their own preferred brand might suffer from loss of quality, meaning they are now in the market for something new.

For these and many other reasons, it can be useful to keep in touch with these casual customers. It may not be efficient but it can be effective. However, the general rule remains that the business should devote the bulk of its time and resources to building relationships with that important 20 per cent of customers.

Now let us look inside the organisation and observe the principle that 80 per cent of value is created by 20 per cent of employees. This principle has been observed many times. Back in the early twentieth century the American engineer Harrington Emerson divided organisations into the 'many' and the 'few'. The 'many' were necessary to get work done, but it was the 'efficient few' who controlled and guided the organisation. We can also recall the paradox of productivity described by Charles Handy (see Chapter 3). Handy argued that globally, more and more productivity is being concentrated in the hands of the few. Thus, although global productivity is rising, the benefits of that productivity are not being distributed equally.

Again, this leads people to suggest that companies should concentrate on those 20 per cent – the innovators, the creators of value – and see the rest as somehow less important. This is the thinking behind the concept of 'core competencies' developed by Gary Hamel and C.K. Prahalad in the 1990s. They argued that companies should concentrate on those few things that they are good at and farm out to others the various support and ancillary functions such as information technology. Hamel and Prahalad argued that this is not just a matter of saving money. Senior managers have only a limited amount of attention to devote to problems and they should concentrate on those that are core to the business. Outsourcing less important functions helps companies to focus on the 20 per cent of things that really matter.

Earlier, Charles Handy had foreseen the possibility of organisations evolving to a 'shamrock' model in which the needs of some parts of the organisation received priority over those of other parts. Handy forecast that one leaf of the 'shamrock' would consist of those workers whose work was deemed central to the business and its purposes. These workers would have permanent contracts and be well paid and well looked after. The second leaf would consist of workers brought in on short-term contracts to perform certain essential tasks, and then let go once their task was complete. The third leaf would be composed of non-essential workers who would receive low pay and little or no training or other attention from top management. Handy did not see this as a positive step. He saw the third leaf in particular as turning into a low-paid, low-skilled, demoralised underclass, with their lack of skills in particular condemning them to remain in this third tier in perpetuity. Today, with the rise of low-paid, part-time work in America and Britain in particular, we may be seeing Handy's vision turning into reality.

But is this really the right way to proceed? Cutting non-essential staff out of the organisation looks like a way of trying to beat the Pareto Principle but, as we observed in the introduction to this volume, the point about these 'laws' of management is that you cannot beat them.

Suppose we take an organisation of 10,000 workers and we deem that 2,000 of them are essential to the organisation. The rest are made redundant, their work farmed out to outsourcing agencies, or are demoted to part-time status. Now, we think, we have an efficient organisation. But according to the Pareto Principle it will quickly become apparent that of those 2,000 remaining, about 20 per cent will be responsible for most of the value creation. So we hive off another 1,600 workers and are left with 400. Then we apply the principle again and reduce the organisation to just eighty workers, and so on. Before long we will have no organisation at all! And meanwhile, as it happened to bicycle maker Schwinn (see Chapter 8), other larger organisations will have taken over our markets.

This is the trap that car maker Austin Rover fell into in the late 1970s. Austin Rover decided that the answer to its economic woes was to reduce the number of models it made and the volume of cars it produced, and then downsize its workforce accordingly to get rid of non-essentials in the organisation. But in doing so, it forgot that car-making depends on volume and economies of scale. Attempting to concentrate on 'essentials' actually led the company further away from what really mattered.

Let us go back to the original point: 80 per cent of value is created by 20 per cent of the work force. True, but we still need that 20 per cent. Very often that is also the margin of value in which our profits are to be found. We cannot sell customers goods that are 80 per cent of what they expect. We need 100 per cent; in these days of tough competition, nothing less will do.

Rather than trying to solve the problem of the Pareto Principle, we need to accept it as it is. We need to embrace the paradox and realise that no matter what we do, it will always be there. Quality engineers know this. If a production line creates 1,000 quality defects each year, concentrating on problems in 20 per cent of the production line could reduce this figure to 200. But within that 200, 80 per cent will still come from 20 per cent of operations, and no matter how small the figures become, the problem remains. A small group of customers may be responsible for most of our profits, but within that small group there will be another even smaller group, and so on. The principle cannot be beaten. We can only live with it and its consequences.

The Pareto Principle means that there will never be such a thing as complete efficiency but then, as we saw in Chapter 3, complete efficiency is not always a good thing. If we turn instead to the principle of effectiveness - ensuring that the organisation meets its goals and delivers on its promises to customers rather than merely operating as efficiently as possible - then we find there is a way to accept the Pareto Principle and make it work for us. At an individual level, some employees contribute more than others and some customers spend more money than others. But true effectiveness looks not only at the individual, but at the collective whole. What is the sum total of value that is created? What is the sum total of our relationship with customers? That, in the end, is the most important measure of all.

Further Reading:

Brocka, Bruce and Brocka, Suzanne (1992) *Quality Management: Implementing the Best Ideas of the Masters*, Homewood, IL: Business One Irwin.

Hamel, Gary and Prahalad, C.K. (1994) *Competing for the Future*, Boston, MA: Harvard Business School Press.

Handy, Charles (1989) *The Age of Unreason*, London: Business Books.

Juran, Joseph M. and Gryna, Frank M. (1993) *Quality Planning and Analysis*, New York: McGraw-Hill.

Chapter 12

Rule of the Span of Control

The concept of the span of control was first formally identified by the Lithuanian engineer V.A. Graicunas in the early 1930s. Earlier writers on military strategy had discussed the concept, and authorities as various as the Florentine statesman Niccolò Machiavelli and the Indian statesman and writer Kautilya (see Chapter 7) had noted that it is important for leaders to choose their subordinates wisely for those subordinates will have much responsibility and authority of their own. Perhaps the earliest ever description of an organisation, the ancient Egyptian papyrus known as the *Duties of the Vizier* written nearly 4,000 years ago, showed how authority and responsibility are devolved within organisations.

The principle is very simple. I start a business as a sole trader. I have, obviously, a high degree of control over my own actions. As the business grows, I begin hiring people. As long as I have only a few people working for me, it is comparatively easy for me to watch them, monitor their activity, give them directions and instructions, and take preventive action if one of them does something wrong. These things have to be done. It would be nice to think that other people will always do the right thing without having to receive guidance or instructions, but practical experience tells us that this rarely happens.

But then the business continues to grow. Soon there are 30 employees, then 50. I do not have eyes in the back of my head, I cannot be everywhere at once; I cannot control their actions. I have to hand over a share of my own control to a much smaller group whose actions I *can* control and monitor, at least to a degree; usually my directors and senior managers. The number of employees rises into the hundreds then the thousands. The senior people around me cannot control them all either and so they have to devolve control to other lower-level managers, and so on. Thus we develop a management hierarchy with control passing down through the various layers.

The rule of the span of control, then, says that each manager can only influence, motivate, monitor, guide, and direct a finite number of people. What this number actually is, is open to debate. In an attempt to reach a definite number Graicunas created a mathematical formula, still known as the 'Graicunas formula', and concluded that the optimal number is four; that is, each manager ought to have no more than four subordinates. More than this, and the level of control becomes sub-optimal. Graicunas also made the point that subordinates within the group will also have relationships with each other, and that controlling and monitoring these indirect relationships between subordinates adds to the complexity of the manager's task.

Later observers felt that Graicunas had underestimated the extent of the span of control, and that managers could easily control the activities of six or eight subordinates. More recently the advent of new forms of communication technology has led to further increases and current thinking is that a span of 15 or even 20 people is not impossible. This shift coincides, probably not by coincidence, with a trend towards 'de-layering' and creating flatter hierarchies in organisations. It follows from the above that if one takes out levels of managerial hierarchy, then the number of reports each manager has will increase. Jack Welch, former chairman of General Electric, complained that his managers had 'too few' reports and then embarked on a process of de-layering to take out some levels of hierarchy and increase the number of reports. GE became a more flexible and effective business as a result of this initiative.

But the rule of the span of control still exists, and managers may well have too many reports as well as too few. Again, this is not just a matter of directly 'controlling' people's actions. It is also a matter of knowing what other people are doing, what decisions they are taking and what the unintended consequences of those decisions might be. This is hard enough in an organisation of a few hundred people. How much harder is it in companies such as GE or Tata, each of which employs about 300,000 worldwide? Large organisations are complex systems and the larger they are, the more complex they become. As we have seen earlier in this book, the greater the complexity, the greater the amount of entropy present in the system, and thus the harder it becomes to exert control.

Whenever we hear of an incident in which a catastrophic failure occurs in business, we can be sure that there has been an issue of control failure. Although the courts are still arguing about the causes of the explosion aboard the BP oil rig *Deepwater Horizon* in 2010 that led to a massive oil spill in the Gulf of Mexico, we may be sure that there was a failure of control somewhere along the line; that accident would not have happened otherwise. The more recent 'Valedmort' fiasco which has cost the bank J.P. Morgan so dearly is most definitely the result of a failure of control. No senior executives knew what was going on until it was too late.

Immediately we begin to discuss control, however, we also run up against another key issue in organisations: namely the issue of power. By 'power', I mean both the power to act on our own account, and the power to influence others to act as we would wish them to. Control and power are closely equated in most organisations, and there is generally an equation between the amount of power that a manager has and his or her ability to carry out tasks successfully. One of the limiting factors of the span of control is the ability to exert power. The further another person is away from us, and the less knowledge we have as to where they are and what they are doing, the more difficult it is to assert power.

Power can be a very positive force. When it is used to bring people together willingly in a common cause it can achieve much good. Think of the power that an excellent coach or a captain has over a sports team, or that a good director has over a film. Power does not have to mean active exertion of control over people's movements and words and thoughts; as we saw in Chapter 3, the Daoists of ancient China argued that the highest form of power lay in doing as little as possible oneself, but making it possible for other people to act. On the other hand power used for selfish ends, to create advantage for oneself rather than the organisation as a whole, can be highly damaging.

When the span of control is exceeded and we have to delegate a certain amount of control to other people, we must delegate power to them at the same time as well. That can be hard to accept. We know that good leaders are people who can delegate effectively and that bad leaders are very often ones who try to cling on too tightly to as much power as possible. It is absolutely essential, when managing or leading, to acknowledge that the span of control exists and learn how when to hand over power – and how much power to hand over – to others.

The Brazilian entrepreneur Ricardo Semler found that in his light industrial company, Semco, it was possible to delegate virtually all of his power. His managers and employees knew what was required of them and could work without direction, even setting their own work schedules and budgets. Semco was, for a time, upheld as a model of radical decentralisation and a 'no hierarchy' company. But this model has not been widely adopted. Most companies remain hierarchical, with power concentrated at the top of the organisational pyramid in exactly the same manner described in the *Duties of the Vizier* 4,000 years ago. Most leaders are afraid to delegate power. Semler was not afraid because he knew he could trust his people but in most organisations those bonds of trust are either weak or absent altogether.

James March and Herbert Simon in their book *Organizations* described businesses as coalitions of factions, sometimes joining forces and sometimes competing with each other but very often seeking power for themselves rather than for the business as a whole. Another scholar of organisations, Chris Argyris, described how factions will work to try to block decisions taken by others within the organisation, including its senior managers, using 'defensive routines' to protect their own position. At Corus – now Tata Steel Europe – in the 1990s, managers in the Dutch operations of the company threatened to take their English counterparts to court because they disapproved of a decision the latter had taken.

It takes a very strong leader to overcome these internal factions and unite the company in a common cause. To do this, the leader requires a great deal of power. Yet, as we have seen, the span of control requires leaders to give up at least some of their power. What is more, the larger the organisation, the more power must be delegated through the hierarchy; yet at the same time, the larger the organisation, the more prone it is to the kind of factionalism that March and Simon describe.

How do we deal with this paradox of power? We have to accept that the span of control exists; it may have increased in recent years but it is still there. The answer is that we need to step away from the idea of 'control' and start looking at the linkages within organisations in different ways.

We referred earlier to two very large multinational businesses, General Electric and Tata, each employing about 300,000 people around the globe. They are organised and structured quite differently. GE has a corporate headquarters and seven different divisions: energy, capital, home and business solutions, healthcare, aviation, and so on. Each of its numerous business units is included under one of these divisions. The seven divisional heads report to CEO Jeffrey Immelt, the heads of the business units report to the division heads and so on down the line. This form of organisation is known as the multi-divisional or M-form organisation and has been around for about a century, having been pioneered by Pierre du Pont first at his family firm, explosives maker E.I. Du Pont de Nemours, and then at General Motors.

Tata, as I have described elsewhere, is much more loosely structured. It is more of a coalition or confederacy of different businesses, linked very loosely by cross-shareholdings and cross-directorships but most of all by a strong corporate brand. The brand and the values and identities that it represents are common to all Tata group companies, even those in very diverse fields of business.

As a result of these different structures - and as a result of GE's fundamentally American culture and Tata's fundamentally Indian one - there are some differences in how they are led. Immelt's predecessor at GE, Jack Welch, was outspoken and voluble, often in the spotlight. J.R.D. Tata and Ratan Tata, by contrast, were much more softly spoken. Yet they resemble each other in that none of the three were leaders who led by exerting control over others. All three were very much consensus leaders. They made their own views known, of course, but they encouraged their staff and managers to arrive at decisions together. They did this because of the span of control. One cannot govern 300,000 people alone. There must always be an element of consensual decision-making.

The political scientist and organisation theorist Mary Parker Follett suggested that the idea of control is an illusion. No one really controls very much in an organisation. What happens instead is coordination: people and resources are brought together and urged to work out their own solutions to the problems that they face. And by and large, if they all share the same values and ideals, and provided that they trust each other, they do. At Tata, because people share the values implicit in the

Tata brand, they know what needs to be done. They use their own initiative when solving problems and creating value and profits for their business units. No one has to lean over their shoulders, no one has to drive them.

How we deal with the span of control and the distribution of power is one of the core principles, perhaps even the first principle, of organisation. Everything else depends on it. The structure of the organisation must first and foremost facilitate coordination, not control. Communication systems and reporting channels must be designed to allow people to talk to each other, not merely listen to orders from above. Accept the span of control and turn instead to solving the problems of coordination. That is the only way to deal with the paradox of power.

Further Reading:

Argyris, Chris (1957) *Personality and Organization*, New York: Harper & Row.

Follett, Mary Parker (1924) *Creative Experience*, New York: Longmans, Green.

Gulick, Luther H. and Urwick, Lyndall (1937) *Papers on the Science of Administration*, New York: Institute for Public Administration. (Contains Graicunas's original paper on the subject, and also an excellent paper by Follett on control.)

March, James G. and Simon, Herbert A. (1958) *Organizations*, New York: John Wiley.

Semler, Ricardo (1993) *Maverick! The Success Story Behind the World's Most Unusual Workplace*, London: Arrow.

Witzel, Morgen (2010) *Tata: The Evolution of a Corporate Brand*, New Delhi: Penguin Portfolio.

Chapter 13

Parkinson's Law

The historian C. Northcote Parkinson wrote in his classic study of bureaucracy that 'work expands to fill the time available for its completion'. Parkinson's Law, as this statement has come to be known, is regarded as one of the key principles of bureaucracy, although it could probably be applied to all organisations and all work. How many contracts are completed ahead of schedule? How many teams submit project reports or proposals before the deadline? How many writers submit books to their publishers ahead of the scheduled date? In all three cases the answer is: very few.

Parkinson's Law has many corollaries in other fields, too. A famous one is the statement that 'consumption of resources expands to meet the supply of resources'. If a department is given a budget of X, then it is pretty much certain that this department will spend X, even if its spending requirements could have been met by a smaller budget. In the nineteenth century the economist William Stanley Jevons proposed Jevons's paradox, which states that efficiencies in the consumption of a resource lead to increased consumption of that resource. Today, while engines are more fuel-efficient than ever before, the consumption of fossil fuels is rising steadily. It would appear that Parkinson's Law is just one part of a much broader set of philosophical and physical principles.

Two further statements by Parkinson show how the process works. The first is that 'officials make work for each other'. In bureaucratic organisations functions tend to multiply and be duplicated. People in positions of power create new tasks and responsibilities for others because this increases their power over others. It also increases their prestige, and hence fulfils their need for self-esteem (see Chapter 4). The second statement is that 'officials multiply subordinates, not rivals'. Managers reinforce their own position by exerting power over others and dominating them, which again protects their own position and reinforces self-esteem. These activities expand to fill the time available, and the more time a manager has on his or her hands, the more he or she is free to exert power and make work for others. And, entropically, the more power the manager is able to exert, the more time he or she has to continue exerting control.

I say 'entropically' because Parkinson's view is that these activities are non-productive and destructive. They pull the organisation away from its original purpose. Self-perpetuation of the bureaucracy itself becomes in time the dominating force; the business no longer works to serve customers, it works to serve itself. Parkinson's Law is, indeed, a practical expression of how entropy works in organisations. As work expands to fill the time available, the actual output of the organisation decreases. Only if the time available decreases will output increase but even here there comes a point when efficiency is lost, because if people are given too little time they will not be able to complete their assigned tasks.

Scientific management, the management philosophy developed by Frederick Winslow Taylor and others in the early twentieth century, was initially meant to help deal with the problem of inefficient work and bureaucracy. Scientific management aimed to identify, as precisely as possible, the optimum time and methods for conducting any task. Although it was originally applied to shop-floor work, over time it was applied to marketing and back office functions as well. In theory, this setting of the parameters for optimum performance should have eliminated unnecessary and wasteful work and duplication of effort.

But Taylor and his colleagues reckoned without human nature. Employers and managers used scientific management as a way of gathering more power to themselves, often at the expense of lower-ranking workers. They pushed workers to do the job faster and faster, often beyond what was reasonable. In the Soviet Union the Stakhanovtsy system, based on scientific management, set near-impossible targets for productivity and then punished workers when they failed to meet them. This did not result in efficiency gains; on the contrary, it led to serious efficiency losses. What is more, the effort of determining and setting optimal times and methods for tasks required companies to hire more staff to conduct measurements and enforce standards. These were not productive staff, not part of the efficient few. Following Parkinson's Law, they created work for themselves and multiplied their numbers. Thus the very measures intended to reduce bureaucracy led to more bureaucracy!

The example of scientific management shows how difficult it is to deal with an established and entrenched bureaucracy within an organisation. Once a bureaucracy has been created, one cannot go back; time's arrow decrees that we have to deal with the situation that has been created. Another feature of bureaucracies is that they are very good at defending themselves: they do not give up without a fight. They are adept at controlling the levers of power and at engaging in defensive routines. The UK and India have one thing at least in common: several times over the past few decades, attempts have been made to reform the civil service and cut the numbers of bureaucrats. All too often the end result of these reform efforts is an actual rise in the numbers of bureaucrats along with a corresponding increase in costs.

The best method is to ensure that bureaucracies never have a chance to get entrenched in the first place. Let us go back to the paradox of decay and growth. If there is in every organisation a tendency towards bureaucracy (entropy), there is also a tendency towards entrepreneurialism and dynamism (growth). The assumption is often made that organisations, including businesses, are conservative in nature and naturally resistant to change, but that is usually only true when the organisation faces no particular challenge or believes itself to be in an unassailable competitive position. Authors such as Tom Peters and Jagdish Sheth have, over the years, warned of the need for a competitive challenge to keep companies on their toes.

Here is a seldom-realised fact: when faced with a challenge, at heart most companies want to change. Their instinct and desire is to respond to the challenge. When rental car company Avis realised that it was number two in the market after its rival Hertz, it adopted the slogan 'we try harder'. Avis took on the role of underdog with relish, and its staff prided themselves on commitment to customer service. They did not take over the number one spot from Hertz, but they created a very good dynamic company along the way.

What holds companies back from change is bureaucracy. Bureaucracies are interested in self-perpetuation, not change. Never mind that the law of entropy states that any unchanging system is bound to decay at an ever-faster rate; when faced with threats bureaucracies close their minds to this and concentrate on defending what they have already, never considering what they might stand to lose elsewhere. Defeating this impulse to stand still and creating a culture where the forces of change and growth can set to work is a key task of the leader. Recall that we saw in Chapter 9 how Andrew Grove saw it as one of his key tasks to ensure that his company, Intel, never stood still and was constantly on the alert for possible changes. Recall how Grove made sharing of knowledge a high priority because knowledge and understanding feed change and encourage growth.

Once a bureaucracy does become embedded, very often the only solution is to root it out by force. IBM in the 1950s and 1960s was a dynamic and fast-moving company, full of change. Managers were encouraged to think the unthinkable and come up with new and exciting ideas. IBM's culture celebrated these entrepreneurs, calling them 'wild geese'. But by the 1980s IBM was a very different company. It had been dominant in its industry for too long, and unchallenged for too long. Inertia had set in, and the bureaucrats had taken power away from the entrepreneurs. 'What happened to the wild geese?' ran the bitter joke in IBM. 'They have all been shot.' By the early 1990s IBM was foundering, with the prospect of going out of business very much a reality. Incoming CEO Louis Gerstner found that the culture of the company had turned against any attempt at reform. It took several hard and painful years, during which hundreds of bureaucratic managers had to be forced from their posts, before IBM turned the corner and was able to grow once again.

One cannot escape from Parkinson's Law – the forces of organisational entropy are always there. Look around at any organisation of any size and you will see signs of formilisation and ritualisation, of managers 'bedding down' in their posts and becoming more concerned about power-seeking than advancing the goals of the company. This tendency cannot be eradicated. It can only be acted against by encouraging the countervailing forces of change.

Further Reading:

Gerstner, Louis V. (2002) *Who Says Elephants Can't Dance?* New York: HarperCollins.

Jevons, William Stanley (1866) *The Coal Question*, London: Macmillan.

Parkinson, C. Northcote (1958) *Parkinson's Law*, London: John Murray.

Sheth, Jagdish N. (2007) *The Self-destructive Habits of Good Companies, and How to Break Them*, Engelwood Cliffs, NJ: Wharton School Publishing.

Sull, Donald N. (2003) *Why Good Companies Go Bad, and How Great Managers Remake Them*, Boston: Harvard Business School Press.

Taylor, Frederick Winslow (1911) *The Principles of Scientific Management*, New York: Harper & Bros; repr. Stilwell, KS: Digireads.com.

Chapter 14

The Iron Law of Oligarchy

The political scientist Roberto Michels observed in 1911 that as organisations grow they become more conservative and less democratic until they become oligarchies, controlled by a small clique who have gathered power to themselves. This condition, says Michels, is inevitable, born out of the 'tactical and technical necessities of organisation'. By joining an organisation – for example, by accepting a contract to work for a company – we submit ourselves to the power of this oligarchy.

We can see this phenomenon all around us. Governments are controlled by cabinet ministers and senior civil servants. Political parties are dominated by senior figures who effectively decide most matters of policy. The established churches are controlled by hierarchies of senior clergy. Country clubs are dominated by small groups of members who sit on key committees. And businesses are dominated by small groups of powerful people – usually, but not always, those who sit in the boardroom.

Michels went so far as to say that the political systems we conceive of as democracies are in fact oligarchies. The very organisation of government offers 'dominion of the elected over the electors'. Ancient Athens is held up as an example of the world's first true democracy – even though it denied the vote to women, slaves and the working classes. But even within the small body of electors in Athens there was a tiny body of men, the oligarchs, who really controlled the city.

Oligarchs are those who, as we saw in Chapter 12, gather power to themselves. Sometimes they do so because they believe this is the best way to serve the organisation; at other times they do so for selfish ends, and sometimes they do so for both. A later thinker, the French sociologist Michel Foucault, argued that one of the reasons oligarchs seek to control power is not so much to use it for their own ends, but to deny its use to others. Foucault saw prisons, for example, as places of punishment not so much for committing crimes but for daring to be different, to stand apart from rest of society. People are sent to prisons, or to other institutions such as asylums for the mentally ill, because they do not conform to the social norms expected by society, and by extension the oligarchs. This may be an extreme position, and I have always felt that Foucault may have been exaggerating for effect. But his point that oligarchies use their power to punish anyone who steps out of line in any way is a valid one. When Socrates challenged the intellectual status quo in ancient Athens, the oligarchs tried him in a court designed by himself and sentenced him to death.

Of course, as readers will remember from Chapter 12, there is the paradox of power: we can only exercise power effectively by giving some of that power away. Oligarchs do not govern alone, nor do they rise to power unassisted; they rely on carefully chosen allies and subordinates who share their view. The Dutch psychologist Manfred Kets de Vries has pointed out that even the most ruthless tyrants achieve and maintain power with the consent of others. Saddam Hussein in Iraq and Muammar Qaddafi in Libya could call on loyal supporters from their own clans to enforce their will. And it is always worth remembering that in Germany, Adolf Hitler used the democratic process to come to power before transforming himself into a dictator. So, too, did Napoleon III in France. The same applies in business situations too. Enron chairman Kenneth Ley relied on a hand-picked team of allies in key positions in the firm to carry out his corrupt policies.

What distinguishes most oligarchs is not so much the fact that they delegate power to some, but how carefully they exclude others and shut them off from power completely. One of the distinguishing features of many oligarchies – though not all, as we shall see – is that a large portion of its members are almost entirely powerless. Michels, and Foucault argue that this includes most of us, most of the time. Even in democratic systems we do not have nearly as much power as the electoral process might lead us to expect. Often we have a limited choice of people to vote for, and often we are choosing between one member of the oligarchy and another. Very often oligarchies deny outsiders the chance to challenge those in power.

According to some observers, the only way to achieve power in an oligarchical organisation is to get inside the oligarchy itself, or at least inside its support group. Make yourself useful to the oligarchy and the oligarchs may notice you and delegate a little of the power to you. That was the view of the French bureaucrat Eustache de Refuge in the seventeenth century. His book *Treatise on the Court* is a kind of survival guide, showing others how to 'climb the greasy pole' and achieve positions of power by various means, fair or foul. He also offers guidance on how to survive attacks by jealous rivals and how to cope with downfall and loss of position. Much more recently, Anthony Jay's *Management and Machiavelli* described the oligarchical tendencies within large business organisations and the struggles that go on between those who have power and those who want to seize it from them.

There are of course a number of similarities between oligarchy and bureaucracy (see Chapter 13), and Michels certainly saw oligarchies as producers of bureaucracy. We should qualify this by saying that in certain situations, oligarchies can avoid being excessively bureaucratic. It all depends on the character and nature of the oligarchs. If we follow the iron law of oligarchy we would have to accept that large businesses such as Intel, General Electric, and Tata are to some extent oligarchies. Yet in all three cases the leadership has recognised the entropic threat posed by excessive bureaucracy and worked to keep the organisations flexible and open. Power is shared much more evenly across the organisation, not just with a chosen few. Large Chinese firms can be very oligarchical in nature with power concentrated in the hands of a tiny number of people, yet often they are also very consultative and 'listening' organisations that take on board what members tell the leadership.

In order to understand why the iron law of oligarchy is not always a threat, we need to look a little further at power in organisations. In his book *Understanding Organisations*, Charles Handy notes that there are different kinds of power. He offers the following classification:

- **Physical power**, which Handy describes as the power of the 'bully or the big man', the ability to impose one's will on others by sheer physical force.
- **Resource power**, the ability to influence the behaviour of others by controlling the resources that they need. Russia supplies vitally needed natural gas to many neighbouring countries, and has several times made veiled threats to 'turn off the tap' if those neighbours

offend Russia. Finance departments exercise control over budgets and can coerce other parts of the company into doing what the finance department wants.

- **Position power**, or 'legitimate power', the power that comes along with a particular post or job title. The chairman of the board has a certain amount of power over the board of directors by virtue of his or her position as chairman; that power is assigned to him or her by the company's constitution or articles of association. Position power gives the holder access to people or information which might be denied to others.
- **Expert power**, which derives from personal knowledge, expertise or experience. Those who have knowledge can often barter that knowledge in exchange for position, payment, or other things of advantage to themselves.
- **Personal power**, or charisma, the ability to influence others through eloquence or force of personality.

Handy goes on to describe a sixth form of power, 'negative power', or the power to do wrong and evil things. I am not convinced that this is a separate category. All five kinds of power above can be used in negative ways. To take the example of personal power, Mahatma Gandhi, Nelson Mandela, and Aung Sang Suu Kyi have all used their personal charisma as a force for good, while Kenneth Ley and Adolf Hitler used theirs as a force for bad. What matters is intent, and how the power is exercised. Again Handy offers a typology of the ways in which power is used to influence others:

- **Force:** we compel people to do what we want using threats or physical force.
- **Rules and procedures:** we create norms and rules and expect others to abide by them, threatening them with punishment if they do not, as per Foucault's view of prisons.
- **Exchange:** we bargain with others, offering them something that is in our power to give if they will in turn respond to our influence and support us (hiring people to work for wages is an example).
- **Persuasion:** we hope to influence others through logical argument, moral persuasion, or charismatic example.
- **Ecology:** we create environmental conditions that will influence the way others behave and think. For example, studies have found that

people exhibit quite different behaviours when offices are rearranged. Even changing the colour of the paint on the walls can have an effect.

Again, all of these uses of power can have both positive and negative effects. If a company's property and workers are threatened by terrorists or gangsters, then it is morally right to ask the police to use force to protect them, or to hire security guards. Rules and procedures are often seen as bureaucratic, but every organisation has to have at least some rules and procedures to help guide people to understand their task and purpose.

Assuming the existence of the iron law of oligarchy and the fact that all organisations turn into oligarchies once they have grown to a certain size, we then need to draw a distinction between 'bad' oligarchies of the kind described by Michels, and 'good' oligarchies. That distinction nearly always hinges on the kinds of power that are used, how they are used and, especially, their ultimate purpose. 'Bad' oligarchies gather power and hoard it. They are keen to deny power to all but their own loyal supporters. They use power in unethical ways, and are more likely to use rules and force rather than persuasion and exchange. They create bureaucracies and, whether they are aware of it or not, increase entropy. They drop anchor and defend the status quo rather than seek evolutionary growth, because growth leads to change and change could threaten the position of the oligarchs.

'Good' oligarchies exert power in order to achieve a commonly agreed end. They act in effect as agents for the other members of the organisation following the concept of servant leadership that we discussed briefly in Chapter 7. They try to ensure that power is distributed evenly, but primarily are concerned with using power positively and for a higher purpose. They promote change because they see this as the best way of avoiding entropy and following the trends in the changing environment around them.

The following may be an apocryphal story, but I like it anyway. A senator in ancient Rome looked out of his window one day to see a great crowd of people rushing past chanting and cheering. He at once ran out of doors after them. 'What are you doing, senator?' a bystander asked. 'There go my people,' replied the senator. 'I must go after them, so that I may learn where they want me to lead them'. Roman senators were, unquestioningly, oligarchs. But this particular oligarch believed that his purpose was to understand and serve the will of the people, not to impose his own will on others.

Much effort is put into breaking down oligarchies and making businesses and other organisations more egalitarian and democratic. The iron law of oligarchy suggests that much of this effort might be wasted. We might do better to concentrate instead on making our oligarchies more responsive and more responsible promoters of positive change rather than defenders of bureaucracy and entropy.

Further Reading:

Foucault, Michel (1977) *Discipline and Punish: Birth of the Prison*, trans. Alan Sheridan, London: Allen Lane.

Handy, Charles (1976) *Understanding Organisations*, London: Penguin.

Jay, Anthony (1967) *Management and Machiavelli*, London: Hodder & Stoughton.

Kets de Vries, Manfred (2007) 'The Spirit of Despotism: Understanding the Tyrant Within', *Human Relations* 59 (2): 195–220.

Michels, Roberto (1949) *Political Parties: A Sociological Study of the Oligarchical Tendencies of Modern Democracy*, New York: Dover.

Refuge, Eustache de (2008) *Treatise on the Court*, trans. J. Chris Cooper, Boca Raton, FL: Orgpax Publications.

Chapter 15

The Peter Principle

The Peter Principle was first formulated in the 1960s by the Canadian psychologist Laurence J. Peter and is generally stated as: 'In a hierarchy, every person rises to the level of their own incompetence.' The principle has been discussed in other forms before; the French courtier Eustache de Refuge, whom we encountered in the previous chapter, noted how some people rise to positions of power based on what they have done, not what they can do, and in his classic work *On the Psychology of Military Incompetence*, Norman Dixon describes how army officers who excel at the company level often fail when advanced to the command of a regiment or brigade.

Peter observed that in organisations of all kinds, promotion nearly always depends on previous track record. Mr Smith is put in charge of a steel works that is suffering from low productivity and low output. Within a year he turns the situation around and the steel works is now outperforming both the rest of the group and the industry average. How should Mr Smith be rewarded? The obvious answer is by promoting him to a higher level, perhaps to head the entire heavy manufacturing division. The reasons for doing so are threefold. First, Mr Smith has done something good for the firm, and it is right that he should be rewarded. Second, he has shown obvious signs of talent, and if he continues to exercise that talent he will benefit the firm still further. Third, if he is not rewarded for having done a good job, he may grow unhappy and leave the company, and others, seeing that Smith receives no recognition for his good services, may grow unhappy and depart too.

The third element does present a problem for companies. In the midst of what many journals and magazines have called a 'war for talent', with the supply of high-potential managers not keeping pace with demand, when a company does find a good manager the immediate instinct is to take steps to keep him or her at all costs. Good managers tend to be ambitious: they seek self-esteem and self-actualisation and look for opportunities to achieve these. Promotion to higher office means recognition for achievements, as well as more access to personal power. Most organisations encourage managers to be ambitious and seek promotion because they believe that the prospect of advancement will lead them to work hard and excel.

So far, so good, said Laurence Peter. But just because Mr Smith performed well when in charge of a steel works, is there any proof that he is fit for the far more complex, challenging and demanding post of head of the heavy manufacturing division? As a steel works manager he was responsible for a variety of operational and human resource issues. As a divisional director he will be required to think about strategic issues, finance, and marketing, as well as about operations on a much broader scale. Can he do it?

The problem, said Peter, is that not only is this question rarely answered, very often it is not even asked. People are promoted on the basis of past successes, and no one bothers to check to see whether they have the requirements for future success. So people are promoted through the ranks, until one day they reach a level where they cannot cope with the demands made on them. They have reached the level of their own in competence: they do not have the skills, knowledge, or experience to meet the demands placed on them. Managers are nearly always aware of this, and suffer a great deal of stress and loss of self-esteem when they realise they cannot do the job expected of them. Ironically, then, rewarding managers by promoting them can end up decreasing their happiness rather than increasing it.

Behind the Peter Principle lies our old friend the law of entropy. Each advance up the hierarchy leads to jobs with higher degrees of complexity, and with complexity comes increasing entropy. Managers who can grow and evolve by expanding their own insights and skills can cope with these higher levels of entropy. But some managers can only grow and evolve so far. When they reach the limits of that growth, entropy begins to take over.

Norman Dixon offers a textbook example of this from the army. Redvers Buller was a British army officer active in the latter part of the nineteenth century. As a captain in command of a company and then a colonel in command of a regiment, he was a great success. He was charismatic, extremely brave, and he looked after his men. His soldiers in turn admired and respected him. During the Zulu War in 1879 Buller won the Victoria Cross, Britain's highest award for gallantry, for single-handedly fighting off a large number of attacking Zulus in order to help some of his soldiers who had been cut off from the rest of the regiment make their way to safety. For this exploit and others Buller became a hero, admired by the army and by the general public. He was rewarded with a rapid promotion to major-general.

Then came another war, against the South African Boers, and Buller was put in command of an entire army. His way of leading men had been to rush to the fore armed with revolver and sword, and lead by example. As an army commander, though, he was required to remain in the rear and direct operations. He had no idea how to do this. Instead he concentrated on trivial details that he *could* control, like the appearance and deportment of his soldiers. On one occasion he ordered men who had lain down on the ground to avoid bullets from Boer snipers to stand up again and expose themselves to fire, so that they would not get mud on their uniforms. His first battle, at Colenso, was one of the worst and most humiliating defeats in the history of the British army. He was fired from his command and a brilliant career ended in failure. Buller had been promoted to the level of his own incompetence.

Examples of this phenomenon abound in the world of business too, but one which has always made a deep impression on me is that of Roberto Goizueta, president of Coca-Cola in the 1990s. In the late 1970s it became clear that the previous president, Paul Austin, was ready to retire. Three candidates for the post were then announced, all Coca-Cola insiders with excellent track records in their own parts of the company. Rather than assessing all three in turn to see who had the necessary talents and competencies to succeed as president, the chief shareholder and 'grand old man' of Coca-Cola, Robert Woodruff, encouraged the three candidates to compete with each other for the post. The most politically adept and ruthless turned out to be Goizueta, who was appointed in 1980.

But neither his previous successes as an engineer in Coca-Cola nor his skills at political infighting proved to be good enough. Soon after Goizueta's appointment, Coca-Cola began to lose market share to its rival, Pepsico. Within a few years Pepsi-Cola had taken over from Coca-Cola as the leading soft drink brand in America. Goizueta's response was a highly risky one: he ditched the company's iconic Coca-Cola brand in favour of a new brand called, not very imaginatively, New Coke. Coca-Cola fans were outraged, the company was buried in an avalanche of bad publicity and market share slid still further. Eventually Goizueta announced that he was 'reversing' the decision and bringing back the old brand – he was, of course, taking a completely new decision with costs and consequences of its own – and New Coke was quietly shelved. It took several years and more expense before Coca-Cola regained its former competitive position. Goizueta lacked the necessary strategic and marketing experience to realise the mistakes he was making, and he seems, strangely for a company insider, to have lacked understanding of the empathic connection between the brand and its consumers.

What can be done about the Peter Principle? Let us be clear about this: while the other 19 'laws' in this book cannot be violated, at least not without a very high risk of negative consequences, this particular rule *must* be broken. It is simply not acceptable to promote people into positions of senior management and leadership for which they are not fit; and yet that is what companies all over the world do, every day.

Most companies would deny that they do this. In fact, I have never yet met a senior executive who admits that this goes on in their own organisation. On the other hand plenty of junior managers, with experience of working under people promoted to the level of their own incompetence, are only too happy to attest to the existence of the Peter Principle.

Companies, especially large companies, have sophisticated assessment systems often involving impartial external assessors, and these systems are designed to ensure that people are promoted on the basis of their ability to do their new jobs. All too often, though, power and politics take over and people lobby for their favourite candidate. And the urge to promote as a reward for past achievements is so strong, for all the reasons described at the start of this chapter, that independent assessments are overridden. I have worked with independent assessors in the past, and I have seen a number of cases where the person who actually got the job was the one that we regarded as least suitable for the post.

Bringing in new blood is another tried and tested method. Letting people know that candidates from outside will be considered, especially for senior positions, sends a warning signal to those expecting to be promoted as a reward for past achievements that they cannot take such promotion for granted.

The most effective way around the Peter Principle, however, is continuous management development, training, and education. Once managerial talent is spotted, it is critical that talented people be given the opportunities to develop and expand their capacities to manage and lead. They need to be prepared for tomorrow, not just rewarded for yesterday. This is an expensive process, not least because not everyone who is developed will necessarily go on to higher things. Some will reach the level of their own incompetence anyway and wash out; others may depart to other firms or other careers. But even if only a small number of truly able top managers come through the process, the reward will exceed the cost.

Do not surrender to the Peter Principle. Do not let personal loyalty and desire to reward people outweigh the needs of the organisation. If the Peter Principle triumphs, you will end up with an organisation run by incompetent unhappy people; then, slowly at first and then with ever-increasing speed, unhappiness and incompetence will spread entropically throughout the organisation.

Further Reading:

Dixon, Norman (1976) *On the Psychology of Military Incompetence*, London: Pimlico.

Greising, David (1998) *I'd Like the World to Buy a Coke: The Life and Leadership of Roberto Goizueta*, New York: John Wiley & Sons.

Peter, Laurence J. (1969) *The Peter Principle*, London: Pan.

Chapter 16

Gresham's Law

The principle popularly known as Gresham's Law states that 'bad money drive out good money'. This is a simplified version of the original law, which, in its initial and more complex formulation, refers to foreign exchange rates and the effect of government attempts to manipulate them. The great sixteenth-century English financier Sir Thomas Gresham referred to this law in his *Memorandum on the Understanding of Exchange*, but his name only became associated with the principle during the exchange rate controversies in the nineteenth century. The fifteenth-century Polish astronomer and polymath Nicholas Copernicus and the fourteenth-century French mathematician Nicole Oresme had also identified this principle.

In the days of metal economies – that is, when circulating money was made of precious metals, usually gold, silver, or copper – a popular method used by governments to increase the amount of money in circulation was to debase the coinage, most commonly by reducing the amount of precious metal in each coin and increasing the amount of base metal such as lead or tin. People were quite aware of this practice, and could tell the difference between debased coins and those with a higher precious metal content. Although governments gave each coin an identical face value, people regarded the coins with high metal content as being of higher value. They would therefore spend or pass on the debased coins whenever they could, and would keep the high-value coins for themselves. Thus the 'good' money would be progressively withdrawn from circulation while the 'bad' money continued to circulate.

Examples of this can still be seen today. Reports in the British media in early 2012 suggested that there are hundreds of thousands of forged £1 coins in circulation. Legally these coins have no value and it is a criminal offence to spend them; they should be handed over to the bank and withdrawn from circulation. However, this means effectively losing money: bad coins cannot be exchanged for good ones. Therefore, whenever people discover they have a fake coin, the usual response is to spend it as soon as possible, passing on the problem to someone else. Bad money remains in circulation.

When Greece joined the newly formed European single currency, the euro, Greek people were supposed to hand over their original currency, drachmas, to the banks in exchange for euros. An unknown amount of money, but probably the equivalent of many millions of dollars worth of drachmas, was in fact withdrawn from circulation as people hoarded what they perceived to be a 'good' currency in the expectation that the euro would turn out to be a 'bad' one. They may yet be proved right. Examples of hyperinflation and other economic turmoil in developing countries often feature the hoarding of safe currencies such as pounds sterling and US dollars while devalued local currencies continue to circulate.

The principle applies to much more than just money. Economist George Akerlof found that in the second-hand car trade in America, so-called 'lemons' – cars with chronic defects – tended to be sold and re-sold while good-quality cars would disappear off the market as people kept them for long periods. Again, we try to keep the quality goods for ourselves while passing the defective ones to someone else. Akerlof referred to this as a problem of 'information asymmetry'. The seller knows the car is defective while the buyer does not; otherwise the latter would not make a purchase. Similarly, under Gresham's Law those who hold bad currency can only pass it on to others if the recipients do not realise it is bad money. If they do, they will charge a discount of the value of the currency or even refuse to accept it altogether.

In Europe, low-cost budget airlines have taken over a large share of the market from higher-priced mainstream competitors, again thanks to information asymmetry. Because tickets are advertised at a very low cost, passengers assume that journeying with a budget airline will be cheaper. However, budget airlines charge extra for things that mainstream airlines include in the ticket price, and there are also additional costs incurred in getting to and from the airports used by budget airlines, which are often a considerable distance from the actual destination. The prices of budget airlines and mainstream airlines are often just about equivalent, but information asymmetry means that passengers fail to check the hidden costs. In the nineteenth century the economist and mathematician Charles Babbage also noted how information asymmetries prevent people from knowing the true cost of quality of what they are buying.

Information asymmetry is not the only force at work, however. There is a kind of entropic force that enables 'bad' actions or behaviour to flourish at the expense of 'good' intentions. Compare Gresham's law to the observations we made in Chapter 6 about the impact of corrupt behaviour. Once a company surrenders to the temptation of paying a bribe, for example, it is then on the hook. Word quickly gets around that this company pays bribes and corrupt officials will then insist on bribes as a matter of course - very often increasing the amount as time goes on. What is more, once this reputation becomes public, honest and ethical companies may refuse to do business with it and cut off relationships, forcing the company deeper into the embrace of the corrupt. Corruption becomes part of the atmosphere the company breathes. Sometimes, as at Enron, otherwise honest people are put under such pressure to behave corruptly that they cave in. Sometimes, as at Satyam, the impact of the scandal when it finally breaks damages people who had not even been aware of the wrong-doing. Corruption drives out ethics.

Bad ideas can also drive out good ideas. Team meetings, unless the team is well motivated and ably led, are a great place to watch this happen. Good ideas are introduced, but instead of debating them on merit, the team adopts a defensive posture and comes up with reasons for rejecting the ideas. This is particularly the case when bureaucracies have taken over and the business is now resistant to change. 'Groupthink', the practice whereby people fall into line with the perceived dominant idea rather than expressing ideas of their own, becomes the order of the day.

In my own work in publishing, I have been involved in publishing meetings when it is proposed that a certain book be published, and heard nine out of 10 people in the room express views solidly in favour. But then the tenth speaks expressing doubts, arguing that there is too much risk. Gradually the other nine began to lose confidence and begin to agree with the tenth: it is risky to publish, it is less risky to do nothing. The book is rejected (in one case, the title was picked up by a rival and went on to sell extremely well).

Bad people also drive out good people. The phenomenon of the 'toxic leader', the term first appearing in the 1990s but the concept well known to Machiavelli and Eustache de Refuge centuries before, has been often described and discussed. Unpleasant, bullying, abusive colleagues and superiors can exert a marked influence on organisations. Some people stand up and fight back, but the instinct of most of us is to get out of the organisation and go somewhere else. Toxic managers can set up a brain drain that quickly robs the business of its best people.

Toxic staff also drives away customers. Restaurants and hotels where the staff is surly and unhelpful, shops where assistants are rude or ignore customers entirely, banks whose call centres are staffed by incompetent people: these are just a few common examples of how staff can create unfavourable impressions in the minds of consumers. Toxic customers also drive other customers away, especially if their behaviour is not restrained by staff. Travelling on business a few years ago, my wife and I stayed at a hotel where 90 per cent of the other guests were what the British refer to as 'chavs': they were alcoholic, loud, rude and used language as foul as I have ever heard in my life – and my father was in the navy. The hotel was clean and comfortable and the food was good, but we left the next morning vowing never to return. The problem was having the wrong sort of customer that drags down the public image of brands as has beset many companies, including fashion retailer Burberry and the beer brand Stella Artois.

Some observers have equated Gresham's Law with the paradox of efficiency and effectiveness (see Chapter 3). Too great an emphasis on efficiency can indeed harm effectiveness. Recall the example of Delta Airlines discussed in Chapter 4. Cost-cutting in order to achieve greater efficiencies led to a collapse in staff morale. The evident unhappiness of the staff led in turn to declining standards of service, which in turn led customers to transfer their business elsewhere. The quest for efficiency ended, for Delta, in bankruptcy.

Gresham's Law, and the versions of it that we have identified here, can be seen as a subset of the law of unintended consequences. The ultimate effect of debasing coins is to slow economic activity, quite the opposite of the impact that was intended. The introduction of a new currency might be intended to stimulate economic growth, whereas in fact it produces the opposite reaction. A new system designed to improve customer service might actually make the service experience worse. The problem is that once these decisions have been taken, they cannot be reversed: time's arrow is in flight, and cannot be returned to the bow from which it was shot. Once a currency is debased, it is debased; there is no remedy except to withdraw it and mint a new one. Once a toxic manager has been hired, the damage is done; firing him or her removes the source of infection but does not heal the wounds already caused.

The best way of ensuring that Gresham's Law does not take effect is to attack the problems at their cause and ensure that the 'bad' does not have a chance to come into existence in the first place. Ensure a supply of sound money, make sure good ideas get a chance to be heard, concentrate on quality, hire good people who are compatible with the organisation and understand the need for customer service, and focus on getting the right customers and discourage those who will harm the business. Do these things and the negative forces will not have a chance to establish themselves. This not to say that life will necessarily be easy; but it will certainly be a lot less difficult.

Further Reading:

Akerlof, George A. (1970) 'The Market for Lemons: Quality Uncertainty and the Market Mechanism', *Quarterly Journal of Economics* 84 (3): 488–500.

Babbage, Charles (1835) *The Economy of Machinery and Manufactures*, London: Charles Knight.

Balch, Thomas Willing (2008) *The Law of Oresme, Copernicus and Gresham*, New York: Read.

De Roover, Raymond (1949) *Gresham on Foreign Exchange*, Cambridge, MA: Harvard University Press.

Lipman-Blumen, Jean (2004) *The Allure of Toxic Leaders: Why We Follow Destructive Bosses and Corrupt Politicians – And How We Can Survive Them*, Oxford: Oxford University Press.

Whicker, Marcia Lynn (1996) *Toxic Leaders: When Organizations Go Bad*, Westport, CT: Quorum Books.

Chapter 17

Martin's Rules

Martin's rules are a set of principles for conducting banking business, although they have implications for financial management and even strategy more generally. They are derived from a document entitled 'Proper Considerations for Persons Concerned in the Banking Business' that Thomas Martin drew up in the aftermath of the South Sea Bubble of 1714–21, a banking scandal that nearly wrecked the British financial system and has strong parallels with the global financial crisis of 2008.

Martin joined the London bank known as the Grasshopper in 1699. The Grasshopper had been founded by Sir Thomas Gresham in the sixteenth century and had for a long time been one of London's leading banks. Martin rose quickly through the ranks, clearly showing aptitude for direction and control, as well as banking. In 1711 he became senior partner and was thus responsible for charting the bank's course through the South Sea Bubble and its collapse. He retired in 1725 to live a life of leisure, still only in his mid-forties, and went on to live to the age of 96, an astonishing feat for those times. The bank was renamed Martin's Bank in his honour and flourished for many years as one of the top 10 banks in Britain until it was bought out by Barclays in 1969.

The South Sea Bubble began when the South Sea Company, a London-based joint stock company, began to buy large portions of the British government's public debt. Shareholders were promised very large returns, as in return for this purchase the government had granted the South Sea Company a monopoly on trade with South America. Shareholders were unaware that the company was badly overstretched (a situation compounded by the fact that huge bribes had been paid to officials in the treasury in order to secure the purchase of the debt), and a brisk trade in shares ensued with the value of South Sea shares being driven steadily upwards.

By about 1719, a kind of mania had begun with all sorts of speculative ventures springing up and their value quickly escalating as people scrambled to get into the market. Many people invested everything they had, mortgaging houses and land to buy shares. Banks also got involved, lending share purchasers large sums of money at high rates of interest and very often with no security apart from the shares themselves. Most of these ventures were fundamentally unsound, and many were frankly fraudulent.

Martin seems to have believed at first that South Sea shares would hold their value and bought them, albeit cautiously. By 1719, he had changed his mind and was urging his clients and all who would listen to avoid shares in the South Sea Company and all other speculative ventures. He found few people prepared to listen to him. The collapse of the South Sea Company in 1721 and the bursting of the financial bubble wiped out many investors and many banks. Although one of Martin's staff had been trading in speculative shares and was arrested for fraud, on the whole the bank had followed his prudent policy. As with Warren Buffett's Berkshire Hathaway during the dotcom bubble of the late 1990s, Martin had played things safely and cautiously.

It was in the aftermath of the collapse of the bubble that Martin sat down and wrote 'Proper Considerations for Persons Concerned in the Banking Business', most likely intended as a guide for his own staff. The purpose of the rules was to remind people of the basic purpose and function of banking and warn them off speculative behaviour. In Martin's rules there are strong overtones of Buffett's Rule, 'never invest in what you do not understand' (see Chapter 8). Various versions of the document appeared over time; the version I have used here dates from 1746 and is reproduced in George Chandler's *Four Centuries of Banking*. I have omitted a few of the rules that refer specifically to financial instruments current at the time. The generic rules are as follows:

1. Some judgement ought to be made of what sum is proper to be lent out at constant interest.
2. Do not lend money without application from the borrower and upon alienable security that may be easily disposed of and a probability of punctual payment without being reckoned difficult by the borrower.
3. All are loans to be paid when due.
4. Do not boast of a great surplus or plenty of money.

5. When loans do not offer to lend on stocks or other securities, buy for ready money and sell for time.
6. To appear cautious and timorous contribute very much to give persons in credit an esteem among mankind.
7. Avoid unprofitable business, especially when attended with trouble and expense.
8. It is certainly better to employ a little money at a good advantage, if lent safely, in order to have a greater cash by you, though possibly you may extend your credit safely.

Rules 1 and 2 are reminders to be prudent. Banks need to know the safe limits of their exposure to the market and should not lend beyond that. They should also not lend unless the borrower (a) can offer genuine collateral and (b) can be reasonably expected to repay the money. The phrase 'without being reckoned difficult by the borrower' is an interesting point. Borrowers are more likely to repay loans if the loan payments are not a massive burden, or in other words, the larger the repayment and interest demanded, the higher the chance of default. Thus what looks like profitable business very often is not. Both rules can easily be reversed; companies should know the amount which is safe for them to borrow and not go beyond that limit, and they should also have a clear idea of the revenue streams that will enable them to find money to repay the loans. Many of the companies that collapsed during and after 2008 were heavily overextended already in terms of borrowing, and the downturn hit their sources of revenue and meant they could not longer pay their debts. Prudent borrowers suffered far less during the crisis.

Rules 4 and 6 are injunctions to be cautious in manner; as well as acting prudently it is necessary to give the appearance of prudence. Thinking back to the South Sea Bubble, Martin suggests that caution and an unwillingness to take large risks will contribute to the reputation and image - in other words, the brand - of a bank. Such a reputation will in turn attract cautious and prudent customers, in Martin's view the right kind of customer. With borrowers and lenders sharing the same values, it ought to be possible to conduct business in a way that is advantageous to both.

Rule 7 follows on from Buffett's Rule. Banks should not get entangled in complex and difficult business from which little or no profit can be expected. Most of all, they should avoid speculative behaviour. After all, the money banks gambled on the markets during the South Sea Bubble and during the housing boom of the 2000s was not ultimately their own but that of their customers, coupled with money they had borrowed from other banks. Once again Martin is reminding banks of their purpose and of the need for frugality and caution.

I have shown Martin's rules to bankers on several occasions. Some have been appalled; with so little appetite for risk, how did Martin ever expect to make profits? Yet he did make profits, and very good ones, good enough to enable him to retire in his forties. Others see the rules as being simple common sense. But in times of irrational exuberance, common sense often gets thrown out of the window, at least until the bubble bursts. I would advise not only bankers but anyone involved in financial markets to keep a copy of Martin's rules close at hand and to remember them when markets start to overheat. Following Thomas Martin's precepts offers a clear road through the dangers and temptations of financial bubbles.

Further Reading:

Chandler, George (1964) *Four Centuries of Banking*, London: B.T. Batsford.

Mackay, Charles (1995) *Extraordinary Popular Delusions and the Madness of Crowds*, London: Wordsworth.

Paul, Helen Julia (2010) *The South Sea Bubble: An Economic History of Its Origins and Consequences*, London: Routledge.

Shea, Gary S. (2007) 'Understanding Financial Derivatives During the South Sea Bubble: The Case of the South Sea Subscription Shares', *Oxford Economic Papers* 59 (Supplement 1).

Chapter 18

Fayol's 14 Points

Henri Fayol was a French mining engineer who wrote an influential early book on management, *Administration Industrielle et Générale*, translated into English as *General and Industrial Management*. Although Fayol's ideas fell out of fashion after the rise of scientific management in the early twentieth century, his basic concept of the functions and duties of a manager have continued to be influential. His 14 points sum up both the duties of the individual manager and the interrelationships between parts of the organisations, and do so in a holistic way. Whereas the scientific managers such as Frederick Taylor concentrated on breaking down and analysing individual tasks, Fayol saw management from the perspective of the whole firm.

Fayol's ideas on management came from long and intensive analysis based in part on his own experience. His engineering education had come at French mining schools strongly imbued with the philosophy of positivism, which held that the only true form of knowledge is that which can be verified and proven as fact using scientific methods. Fayol went on to become a talented engineer, responsible for several important innovations but, as he said himself, he became a far better manager than he was an engineer. Taking over as managing director of a failing mining company in 1888, within a few years he turned it around. The company, Commentry, Fourchambault et Decazeville, became one of the largest iron and steel producers in France. Fayol continued to lead the company for more than 30 years.

Analysing the things that managers need to do if they are to be successful, Fayol came up with a list of five tasks. The American writer Luther Gulick took Fayol's original idea and expanded the list to seven tasks for which he developed the acronym POSDCORB: Planning, Organising, Staffing, Directing, Co-ordinating, Reporting, and Budgeting. Essentially, Fayol argued that managers should first decide *what* should be done (planning, organising), then determine *how* it should be done and what resources would be used (staffing, budgeting), and then oversee the implementation and make certain that the process stays on track (co-ordinating, directing, reporting). The purpose of management is to ensure that others work together to achieve commonly held goals in a coherent and effective manner.

The POSDCORB concept has had its critics. In his classic study, *The Nature of Managerial Work*, the Canadian scholar Henry Mintzberg argued that the scheme is too neat and too orderly. What managers actually do, says Mintzberg, is rather messy and not easily categorisable. Managers talk to people, they react to situations as they happen, they make decisions as often as not based on instinct as on reason. Very little of what they do can be categorised as planning, organising. Mintzberg's own detailed studies of managerial behaviour and actions back up his conclusions. But powerful though Mintzberg's arguments are, we have to ask a question: just because managers do behave in this way, does it mean that they *should* behave in this way? My colleague Jacques Kemp, a former senior executive at ING, has made the point that while companies invest millions in management control systems for production, marketing, supply chains, and so on, they invest nothing in management control systems for management itself. Management is still done in an ad hoc, amateurish way and that, says Jacques, is one of the reasons why so much management is so inefficient.

Certainly POSDCORB has had its supporters, too. Chester Barnard's *The Functions of the Executive*, one of the most influential management books of all time, acknowledged that managerial work is 'fuzzy' in nature and hard to define precisely, but still took the view that managerial activity can be broken up into sets of tasks much as Fayol had described. Other contemporary writers such as Lyndall Urwick and Albert Lepawski agreed.

We have discussed POSDCORB because it is a good introduction to Fayol's mindset. It shows us what he thought the purpose of management is. Management, according to Fayol, is about getting things done, and the three stages he defined – deciding what is to be done, deciding what resources will be needed, and then coordinating activity and checking on progress to ensure that it actually does get done – still have to be followed whether one is acting in a planned and formal way or in a completely ad hoc manner. None of the three stages can be ignored.

The 14 points are intended to describe the fundamental principles on which management rests. All 14 of these are things that organisations and their members need, even if their exact nature changes over time.

1 **The division of labour.** Long ago the philosopher Plato, in *The Republic*, noted how any complex society relies on the division of labour. As soon as we move beyond the level of mere subsistence we find specialists who have certain skills and do certain things the rest of us cannot do. Karl Marx later argued that there are specialists in 'knowledge work' as well as in manual labour. All organisations rest on the principle of the division of labour and, so long as people work at tasks for which they are qualified and have the requisite knowledge and skills, those organisations will be stronger as a result. As Adam Smith pointed out in *The Wealth of Nations*, the combined effort of many specialists, if wisely directed, will be greater than the sum of its parts. Management exists to ensure that labour is divided and then recombined in the most effective manner, so that everyone works together to achieve the organisation's purpose.

2 **The establishment of authority.** Recall the discussion of power in Chapter 14. Managers are in effect an oligarchy. It is up to them whether they become a bureaucratic oligarchy that uses authority to gather power to themselves for selfish ends, or whether they become a benign oligarchy that directs power for the ultimate good of the organisation, its members, and society as a whole.

3 **The enforcement of discipline.** This does not mean disciplining and punishing those who step out of line, though in some organisations this is indeed what happens. Fayol is talking of here of something akin to the concept of academic 'rigour', a discipline of habits and minds that leads people to work at the optimum level of both efficiency and effectiveness, getting the job done while minimising waste. And of course, even in the most benignly managed organisation there is a need for rules and discipline to stop people from behaving in anti-social or unethical ways, breaching health and safety rules, disclosing sensitive information, even engaging in criminal activities that can impact on the company's image and reputation. These forms of discipline are necessary to protect the organisation and its members.

4 **Unified command.** Fayol argued that no employee should report to more than one supervisor, so that the employee knows with absolute clarity what he or she is expected to do. Some modern forms of organisation, such as matrix organisations, break this rule. In matrix organisations people will often have two or more reports, for example to the head of a functional department and the head of a project team. On the other hand, one of the common problems reported in matrix organisations is confusion when the two supervisors give conflicting sets of instructions. The principle of 'unified command' should be taken to mean that both supervisors act in harmony and do not conflict with each other. We could rename this point 'clarity of purpose' if we chose.
5 **Unity of direction.** All control, says Fayol, should emanate from one source. This could be taken to mean that there is one dominant controlling figure who rules the organisation like a king. But that 'source' does not have to be a person. It can just as easily be a concept or a set of values. At the Tata group, the corporate values and code of conduct along with the brand serve together as a device which gives unity of direction. Managers who are confused as to what to do in a certain situation can refer to those values for guidance, and often they do. And unity of direction is important if the company is not to waste effort and resources by engaging in activities not vital to its central purpose.
6 **Subordination of individual interests to the interest of the organisation.** Again, it might appear on the surface as if Fayol is arguing that people are less important than the organisation, that they should surrender power to the organisation. But the more correct interpretation is that Fayol is again referring to that need for unity of direction. At steelmaker Corus in the 1990s, the English and Dutch parts of the company engaged in a damaging argument over the future direction of the business. Each wanted to pursue a course that benefitted its part of the company and its managers, even if that course was detrimental to the interests of the other part. Neither stopped to consider the interests of the company as a whole largely because Corus was created by a not particularly successful merger, and the English and Dutch sides still owed primary loyalty to themselves and their colleagues, and not to Corus. Managers and staff do not have to lose their identity within the company, as

happens at some Japanese firms. But they do need to remember that the success of the company is the purpose for which they came together in the first place.

7 **Fair remuneration for all.** A fair day's work for a fair day's wages remains one of the fundamental principles of organisations. People should be rewarded in proportion to what they put into the company, to the value that they create. There are various means of doing so. The English department store owner John Lewis felt so strongly that his employees were the real creators of value in the company that he handed over ownership to them, dividing it into equal shares that were then given to each employee. Others engage in profit sharing or other schemes that reward employees, or simply pay good wages. When considering fair remuneration, however, recall the hierarchy of needs (see Chapter 5) and understand why people work and what motivates them to come to work.

8 **Centralisation of control and authority.** This point has been challenged in recent extent, but power has to have a source, just as the sun's heat and light have a source. Somewhere there needs to be a source of power in every organisation - and again, this can be a guiding principle or ideal, not necessarily a person. The central authority can be the moral authority of an idea, not the personal authority of a man or a woman. And there must be someone with whom the buck stops, someone who takes charge in a crisis and accepts ultimate responsibility for failures.

9 **A scalar hierarchy, in which each employee is aware of his or her place and duties.** Again, we live in an era in which flatter hierarchies are now favoured, but the rule of the span of control (Chapter 12) tells us that there will always be some hierarchy (and the iron law of oligarchy, Chapter 14, suggests that people will tend to create a hierarchy if one does not yet exist). People need to know what is expected of them and what their own role is in terms of the larger picture, the organisation's purpose. Study after study has found that once employees are aware of what is expected of them, they work harder and are more committed. Vagueness of intent leads to confusion and demoralisation, and ultimately to entropy.

10 **A sense of order and purpose.** Organisations and their members need a sense of purpose, a sense that what they are doing matters

and is worthwhile. Maintaining that guiding purpose and communicating it is a key managerial task.

11 **Equity and fairness in dealings between staff and managers.** Organisations need to move away from the adversarial, white collar/ blue collar, them/us approach to management. Both sides need each other, and both must work together if the organisation's goal is to be achieved. The rule of yin and yang (see Chapter 3) suggests that organisations succeed best when managers and staff regard each other as complementary, not as adversaries. Fairness and trust in relationships are essential if this is to be achieved.

12 **Stability of jobs and positions.** Fayol was not in favour of 'churn' or high turnover of staff and managers. While a certain degree of turnover is necessary in order to bring in new blood and new ideas, excessive churn is not only expensive in terms of recruitment and training costs but also results in a brain drain as useful knowledge and ideas flow out of the organisation. Managing people so that the right people are in the right jobs is a fundamental principle of management.

13 **Development of individual initiative on the part of managers.** We saw above that Fayol's ideas on control and discipline are based on a need for unity of purpose and coordinated working together. Here he shows his awareness of the rule of the span of control. A key element of management is encouraging subordinates to take responsibility and become better managers in their own right, using delegated power more effectively.

14 **Esprit de corps and the maintenance of staff and management morale.** Maintaining a positive spirit and a sense of moving forward, coupled with a confidence that the company's purpose will be achieved in the end no matter what obstacles stand in the way, is an absolute essential of management. Today we would refer to this as 'motivation', and if you pick up almost any textbook on management or leadership you will find that 'motivating others' is seen as a fundamental responsibility. 'Getting things done through other people, willingly', is how British leadership guru John Adair defines leadership. Management is not about pushing or driving other people to do things. It is about ensuring that they do them willingly, because they want to and because they see the purpose and value in doing so.

Although Fayol described the functions of management, he believed absolutely that management had to have purpose. The notion of purpose, which he was one of the first to describe, is fundamental to good management. Without purpose, as managers we merely go through the motions. That same point was made by one of the twentieth century's great writers on management, W. Edwards Deming.

Further Reading:

Barnard, Chester I. (1938) *The Functions of the Executive*, Cambridge, MA: Harvard University Press.

Brodie, Morris B. (1967) *Fayol on Administration*, London: Lyon, Grant & Green.

Fayol, Henri (1984) *General and Industrial Management*, New York: David S. Lake.

Kemp, Jacques, Schotter, Andreas and Witzel, Morgen (2012) *Management Frameworks*, London: Routledge.

Lepawski, Albert (1949) *Administration: The Art and Science of Organisation and Management*, New York: Knopf.

Mintzberg, Henry (1973) *The Nature of Managerial Work*, New York: Harper & Row.

Urwick, Lyndall (1937) 'The Function of Administration', in Luther Gulick and Lyndall Urwick (eds), *Papers on the Science of Administration*, New York: Institute of Public Administration.

Chapter 19

Deming's 14 Points

The American engineer W. Edwards Deming is regarded as one of the founders of the quality movement in business. His argument that businesses could become more profitable, more efficient, more effective, and more socially responsible if they concentrated on quality and eliminated wastes took a long time to catch on. It is now universally recognised as true.

As an engineering student, Deming took a summer job at the American telephone equipment maker Western Electric. Here he worked with the mathematician Walter Shewhart, who was researching methods of quality control. Shewhart drew many ideas from the British mathematician and biologist Ronald Fisher who had developed methods of measuring statistical variances in plant species as they mutated and evolved, and applied these same methods of measuring variances to assembly line production; the method became known as statistical quality control (SQC). Fisher, in turn, was a disciple of Charles Darwin and his theories of evolution (see Chapter 2) and so, indirectly, Darwin is responsible for the modern quality movement.

Following the Second World War, Deming and his fellow engineer Joseph Juran became consultants to Japanese companies. Japan's industries had been largely destroyed by American bombing raids during the war and there was now a rush to rebuild. Japanese companies had been very interested in quality for some time, and companies such as Toyota had been pioneers in developing quality control systems. There were already a number of important Japanese thinkers on quality management including Kaoru Ishikawa and Taiichi Ohno, the latter responsible for much of the quality management system at Toyota. These men and others found Deming's ideas on quality control very valuable. Although both Deming and Juran were always careful to point out that they did not invent the idea of quality control in Japan, their Japanese counterparts have given them much credit for developing the movement there. And, as James Womack and Daniel Jones pointed out in their book *The Machine That Changed the World*, it was the quality movement that helped propel Japan into the position of a world-class manufacturing centre and grow to be the second largest global economy (a position it has only recently surrendered to China).

However, Deming was more than just a statistician and engineer. He never wavered in his view that statistical proof was the most important kind of evidence, and in this respect he resembled Fayol the positivist. 'In God we trust', he once said, 'all others must bring data.' But he also realised during his time in Japan that SQC and quality control methods were not enough to ensure quality. There also had to be a mindset, an acceptance that quality mattered, and a genuine desire to achieve it. Another well-known writer on quality, Philip Crosby, advanced the view that 'quality is free' and advanced a logical argument for the case that investments in quality management systems would always be paid back by corresponding efficiency savings, lower levels of waste, and higher customer satisfaction. But Deming knew that managers do not always listen to logical arguments and are all too prone to give in to short-term self-interest.

In his book *Out of the Crisis*, his attempt to advise American business leaders and policy makers on how to respond to the competitive threat from Japan – a threat which, ironically, he had helped create – Deming argued for a complete cultural change and a new approach to management. Like Fayol 80 years before him, Deming came back to the purpose of management. What is management for? What is it meant to do? What are its fundamental elements? He and Fayol came at the subject from different angles: Fayol the European positivist started from the perspective of the whole organisation and, as we have seen, argued that individuals must respect the needs of the organisation; Deming, as we shall see in a moment, put the focus more firmly on the individual. The ultimate end of management, he argues in effect, is to give people the ability to take purposive action, and like Fayol, purpose plays a prominent role among the 14 points listed in *Out of the Crisis*. These are:

1 **Create constancy of purpose.** Organisations and their members need constantly to remember why they are doing what they do, and one of the key roles of management is to keep that purpose in front of people and remind them of it.

2 **Adopt a new philosophy for leadership and purpose.** In turn, that need to drive purpose needs to shape how managers view themselves and their own role. Management is not about hitting targets but about creative value and satisfying social needs. Deming was one of the first to point out that it is the customer, not the manufacturer, who defines what 'quality' is. If a product or service adds value for the customer, then it is good quality. Management is there to help employees satisfy customer needs, not to achieve its own selfish ends.
3 **Cease dependence on inspection to achieve quality; build quality into the product in the first place.** Prior to the work of Deming and Juran, quality had been achieved by inspecting products as they came off the production line, throwing out the defects and sending the rest on to the customer. Although this resulted in customer satisfaction, there was often a high degree of waste. Deming's view, and that of Ohno and the Toyota engineers, was that if the production systems were correctly designed in the first place, defects could be reduced or even eliminated entirely. The emphasis needed to be switched from the products to the system that made them. Modern quality initiatives such as Six Sigma grew out of this way of thinking.
4 **End the practice of awarding business on the basis of price; consider the total cost of good and bad quality.** This is similar to the principle advocated by Crosby, that quality is free. Paying low prices for goods that turn out to be defective or have a short life span is a false economy. Deming's view is that investing in quality will always pay.
5 **Undertake continuous improvement of both production and service.** The idea of continuous improvement comes from the Toyota system. The guiding philosophy is that no system is ever perfect, and no matter how good it may be, improvement is always possible. But there is also an element of Darwin's Rule here (see Chapter 2). Things change: new technologies are invented, customers demand new features on products, new environmental regulations must be obeyed. No production system lasts forever and constant updating and change must be a feature.
6 **Institute training on the job.** Deming is arguing here for what we now know as continuous learning. Just as systems need to constantly change and update, so do people; there is constant pressure to learn

and grow in order to achieve full effectiveness. People need to learn from and through their work so that they may continuously improve.

7 **Institute leadership.** Management is about much, much more than simply managing processes. Managers need to be leaders. They need to motivate, inspire and enthuse others to grow, change, develop, innovate and drive the company forward.

8 **Drive out fear, enabling everyone to work effectively for the company.** This point has caused some controversy, with Deming's contemporary Joseph Juran arguing that a measure of fear can be healthy – people may be encouraged to work hard if they are afraid of the consequences if they do not. Deming's view, though, is that encouraging people to work out of fear is a 'push' factor, and will never be as effective as the 'pull' factor of wanting to do the job. Compare two workers: one works because he knows that if he does not work, bad things will happen; the other works because she knows that if she does work, good things will happen. Who will be the most productive, effective, and creative? Deming argues that it will always be the latter.

9 **Break down barriers between departments.** As we have seen, knowledge facilitates growth and change and is the answer to entropy. Knowledge enables Andrew Grove's 'paranoid' companies to survive. Breaking down the walls between departments encourages effective communication and allows knowledge to be shared right across the company, enabling the whole company to be more flexible and responsive.

10 **Eliminate slogans, exhortations, and targets.** Deming felt that targets are illogical; the need for continuous improvement reminds us that we can never stop. Targets, on the other hand, encourage people to think that once they have reached the target they can then stop and rest on their laurels, when in reality they can do no such thing. Targets, like slogans urging people to work hard and waste less, can also be coercive, fear-inducing measures. Again, the answer is to give people reasons to want to achieve, and the space in which to achieve.

11 **Eliminate work standards, quotas, management by objectives, and management by numbers; replace these with leadership.** This, again, relates to the point made above. Interestingly, a man who made his name working with standards and management by

numbers is urging their abandonment, at least as a way of measuring performance by progress. All the things he lists in this point, Deming believes, lead to a mechanistic culture of checklists and box-ticking in which managers and workers need only to follow step-by-step plans to achieve success, filling in the colours in a paint-by-number picture in hopes of creating a masterpiece. The real world is far more complex than that. The task of the leader is to motivate and encourage people to achieve success by the routes that they themselves deem possible and that are right and practical for the time and place.

12 **Remove the barriers that rob workers of the right to workmanship, both on the shop floor and in management.** Many contemporaries felt that mass production had robbed workers of pride in their work. Unlike craft workers who felt a genuine sense of creative connection with the products they made, assembly line workers were mere cogs in a machine. Deming's experience in Japan showed him that this was not true. At Toyota, and elsewhere, workers had a very real pride in their work, and there was a sense that shop floor workers and managers shared a common purpose and values. However, the coercive methods in use in many workplaces where workers were driven to work out of fear robbed people of this pride. Quality could only be restored if workers felt personally engaged with the products they made and truly wanted to 'build in' quality.

13 **Institute a rigorous programme of education and self-improvement.** Along with the need to learn from the workplace, Deming also felt that it was important for workers and managers to expand their minds in other ways. The idea of self-improvement and personal betterment is particularly important and we can link this to the needs for self-esteem and self-actualisation (see Chapter 5); helping workers to become better people means that they will also work more effectively.

14 **Put everyone in the company to work to accomplish the transformation.** Like Juran and Crosby, Deming believed that quality is everyone's business. Everyone who works for an organisation has a stake in its success, a reason for wanting that business to do well. The more people put their shoulder to the wheel and push, the more likely that success is.

On that final point, Deming once again shifts the focus back from the individual to the organisation. The need for everyone to contribute if success is achieved is a reflection of his view that the whole is greater than the sum of its parts; people working together can achieve more than the same number of people working independently (which takes us back to Fayol's first point, the division of labour). It may also have been a reflection on personal experience of companies where, according to one variant of the 80/20 rule, a small number of people did most of the work and the rest were passengers who did little or nothing. One earlier observer, the Canadian consultant and writer Herbert Casson, once remarked acidly that it is better to replace a 'do-nothing' director and put a bag of sand on his office chair, on the grounds that the bag of sand will do less harm.

When we look at Deming and Fayol and compare them to each other we see more paradoxes: a paradox of freedom and control, a paradox of the organisation and the individual. Too much control gives us the iron law of oligarchy; bureaucracies in which power is controlled by the few and the many are disenfranchised and powerless. Too much freedom gives us people going in the directions they choose, not those the organisation needs; the results can be loss of focus, diffusion of effort, working at cross-purposes, even anarchy. Organisations are meant to focus the efforts of the individuals towards a goal, but they can do so only if individuals voluntarily submit to some form of control over themselves. But are the rights of the individual then subordinate to the rights of the organisation?

To understand these paradoxes we need first of all to give up on the 'either/or' approach to these problems. The rights of both the individual *and* the organisation are important, and neither must trump the other. Both control *and* freedom are essential; the need – and this is one of the fundamental tasks of management – is to find a yin-yang balance between them so that both are seen as halves of the same whole. Taken separately, neither Fayol nor Deming has the whole truth; one privileges the organisation over the individual, the other believes the organisation is at the service of the individual and that individuals are the true creators of quality and value. In fact, both views are simultaneously valid and true. Individuals and organisations do need each other and depend on each other absolutely. Without each, the other would have no meaningful existence.

Learning how to manage that paradox is the ultimate test of the manager. How is it done? The next chapter will hopefully offer some answers.

Further Reading:

Crosby, Philip B. (1979) *Quality Is Free: The Art of Making Quality Certain*, New York: McGraw-Hill.

Deming, W. Edwards (1986) *Out of the Crisis*, Cambridge, MA: MIT Center for Advanced Engineering Study.

Gabor, Andrea (1990) *The Man Who Discovered Quality*, New York: Times Books.

Ishikawa, Kaoru (1989) *Introduction to Quality Control*, London: Chapman & Hall.

Kanter, Rosabeth Moss (1989) *When Giants Learn to Dance*, New York: Simon & Schuster.

Mahalanobis, P.C. (1948) 'Walter A. Shewhart and Statistical Control in India', *Sankhya: The Indian Journal of Statistics* 9 (1): 51–75.

Ohno, Taiichi (1988) *Toyota Production System: Beyond Large Scale Production*, Cambridge, MA: Productivity Press.

Rudra, Ashok (1998) *Prasanta Chandra Mahalanobis: A Biography*, New Delhi: Oxford University Press.

Womack, James P., Jones, Daniel T., and Roos, Daniel (1990) *The Machine That Changed the World*, New York: Macmillan.

Chapter 20

Drucker's Rule

In several works, notably *The Practice of Management* and *The Effective Executive*, Peter Drucker offers his rule: 'The only valid purpose of a business is to create a customer'. Businesses do not exist to perpetuate themselves, they do not exist to create value and return dividends to shareholders, they do not even exist to create jobs for employees. They exist to serve customers. If they do not serve customers, then they cannot create jobs or generate profits – or indeed, survive. Everything else is subordinate to that one purpose: serving customers.

Drucker's name will already be known to many readers. Born in Austria before the First World War, he worked as a journalist in Germany, then left the country abruptly after publishing a magazine article critical of Adolf Hitler. He worked for several years in Britain as an investment banker before migrating to America where he became a lecturer and a respected and revered writer. Although he explored many themes in his books and articles, the need to serve customers is one that he returned to over and over again.

Drucker uses a curious phrase, 'to create a customer'. We are entitled to ask what he means by that, especially as he himself never really defined the term. I have always interpreted this term in the following way: it is not enough to sit and wait for customers to come to us. We have to go out and seek potential customers and make them aware of the goods and services that we can offer and the value we can add to their lives. If we can do this successfully, then we will have created customers, and so long as we can continue to do so, those customers will return to buy our goods and services.

Other authorities agree. For example, in their recent book *Beyond the Familiar*, Patrick Barwise and Seán Meehan argue that companies which enjoy long-term success are those that meet customer needs consistently, day in and day out, year in and year out. And because customer needs are constantly shifting and changing, companies have to constantly evolve and grow along with their customers. There is an evolutionary process at work here, one that sees customers and companies growing symbiotically and sympathetically alongside each other.

To fully understand Drucker, one needs to know the context of his statement. Drucker believed passionately that free enterprise was a force for good in society. A follower of the economist Joseph Schumpeter, he agreed with the latter's view that entrepreneurs created value not just for themselves but for society as a whole. They generated prosperity, and prosperity in turn was one of the routes by which people achieved freedom. Drucker observed the higher consumption rates of the free societies of the West, and believed that freedom was in part a result of higher levels of economic activity. Founding, owning, and managing a business was therefore a righteous act, one that benefitted the whole of society.

In stating this belief, Drucker was not saying anything new. I have argued elsewhere that this idea can be traced back to the Middle Ages, to Christian scholars such as St Thomas Aquinas and Muslims including Abu Fadl al-Dimashqi and Ibn Khaldun. Merchants and traders played a key role in early Islamic society and many of the early caliphs came from trade backgrounds; the Prophet Muhammad himself was involved in trade and his first wife Khadijah was a successful businesswoman. Al-Dimashqi was one of many early scholars arguing that trade benefitted society as a whole, provided it was conducted in an ethical and honourable fashion and merchants redistributed the money they earned rather than hoarding it for themselves.

In Christian thought, Thomas Aquinas urged the view that merchants help make society happy by providing the goods and services that people need; thus merchants contribute to the sum total of happiness. In satisfying these needs, merchants are entitled to make profits as a reward for the risks that they run. A century or so later the Muslim writer Ibn Khaldun made almost exactly the same point. Zerbanoo Gifford, a British Parsi writer and scholar, makes the same point about Zoroastrianism and believes this philosophy is still strongly present in the Zoroastrian-descended business families such as Tata and Godrej. Much the same philosophy is present in the writings of the post-Second World War Japanese industrialist Konosuke Matsushita who set forth his view that making consumer goods plentiful and cheap would raise the overall standard of living, lift people out of poverty, and increase the sum total of human happiness.

The purpose of business, then, is to provide goods and services that society needs. How does this process happen? Orthodox economics assumes that all human beings are rational agents who seek at all times to maximise our own self-interest. If that were true, then people would always know exactly what they wanted and when they wanted it, would seek out the necessary goods and services through the most effective channels and then make purchases accordingly. In fact, it is not that simple. First, irrational behaviour and changing needs (Chapter 5) mean we are not always rational about our needs and do not always pick the best methods of satisfying them. Second, information asymmetries (Chapter 16) mean that we are not always aware of the most advantageous channels. One of the tasks of marketing is to reduce those information asymmetries and make customers aware of what is available to them.

When we talk of information asymmetries, we come to another paradox. It has been observed many times that the people who most need goods and services to lift their standard of living are the ones that have the most difficulty accessing those goods and services. The middle and upper classes, thanks to better education and training and better access to existing resources, are better able to make comparisons between offers and choose the one that best suits their needs. The poor tend to have more limited choices. In Chicago around 1900 economists found that poor immigrant families were actually paying more for food, purchased from local traders, than wealthy families elsewhere in the city who knew how to shop around for bargains. Similar studies in India, and elsewhere in Asia, have found that the poor often pay more for goods such as soap than their more affluent neighbours.

As the late C.K. Prahalad pointed out in his book *The Fortune at the Bottom of the Pyramid*, there is an immense marketing opportunity awaiting companies that can make goods available, profitably, at prices that poor people can afford. Some companies, such as Tata Beverages and Hindustan Lever in India, are already leading the way in this respect. I would argue that there is no magic about taking this approach. This is the fundamental heart of marketing: providing goods and services to people that enhance the quality of their lives. What Hindustan Lever and Tata Beverages are doing, in terms of redesigning packages and producing smaller units and driving costs down, is what every company should be doing, everywhere, in every market. It is not only a matter of selling to the poor, to those living at subsistence level needing food and shelter. At every level of the hierarchy of needs there are people with needs to be satisfied, and the needs for self-esteem and self-actualisation are no less worthy or less valid than the needs for food and safety.

It has been argued that modern marketing has created the boom in consumer goods that is currently putting pressure on resources and threatening sustainability. I personally believe it is the other way round, that the rise in global prosperity and the swelling numbers of the middle classes has put pressure on modern marketing to supply the goods and services people demand in order to satisfy their needs (although I accept that there is an element of the chicken and the egg here). If we are going to create a sustainable world, the argument goes, we need to reduce demand and reduce consumption; but marketing exists in order to stimulate consumption. Another paradox? Not really. The role that marketing has to play becomes more important than ever. Once again marketing can help to educate customers by offering them sustainable goods and services that they might not have known existed. In Europe, energy companies now routinely offer customers advice on how to save energy (one executive I know estimates that there is more money to be made in helping people save energy than there is in generating and providing energy, though I think we must also be aware of Jevons's paradox (see Chapter 13).

So what do businesses do? They create customers. They communicate information about what they have to offer, and what value people can expect to derive from those goods and services, over and above the cost of purchase. If they do so ethically and honestly – and this is of course a big 'if' – then what they do is moral and right. They are helping society.

What is more, that is the purpose for which businesses were created in the first place. If we go back to the dawn of civilisation, we find that the very first businesses were created to supply needs that people cannot supply for themselves. People traded surpluses of goods they had for goods they did not have, and the net result was an increase in both prosperity and happiness. In *The Republic*, Plato argues that this is one of the essential features of civilisation. We are forced to conclude that businesses exist to serve society - not, as so many managers and business leaders seem to believe, the other way around.

And if we accept this fundamental position, then we have found a way of closing the circle. We can accept the paradox of entropy and growth; we can solve the apparent contradiction between Fayol and Deming. Both men have part of the answer: it is individuals *and* organisations that matter, not individuals *or* organisations. The two depend on each other to meet their goals. Organisations enable individuals to function much more effectively; individuals combine their efforts to make organisations function efficiently. Management and the worker operate in symbiotic fashion to meet the ultimate goal: serving customer needs. Never mind that 80 per cent of the effort comes from 20 per cent of the workforce; instead of bemoaning this fact, we should celebrate that vital 20 per cent of extra effort from the majority that enables us to add the score up to 100.

Deming spoke of involving everyone in the effort. He was right. If everyone gets involved in the drive for quality and service, if everyone takes pride in serving customers and in so doing makes a contribution to society, then businesses stand a good chance of fulfilling their ultimate purpose. The reverse is also true. If businesses turn their back on Drucker's rule and focus only on the selfish ends of themselves or their shareholders, then eventually - the length of time depending on the degree of information asymmetry - customers will realise this and will take their business elsewhere. Then growth will cease, and entropy will increase and multiply.

As a manager, the choice is yours. Recognise that there are fundamental precepts, some of them rooted in the business world, some of them derived from the universe beyond, that are always active and always present in your working life. Respect those principles, find ways of understanding them, and then make that understanding work for you. Alternatively, deny the existence or the efficacy of these precepts and carry on as you wish to do. Then, get ready to pay the price for that denial.

Further Reading:

Barwise, Patrick and Meehan, Seán (2011) *Beyond the Familiar: Long-term Growth Through Customer Focus and Innovation*, San Francisco: Jossey-Bass.

Drucker, Peter F. (1954) *The Practice of Management*, New York: Harper & Row.

Drucker, Peter F. (1967) *The Effective Executive*, New York: Harper & Row.

Kotler, Philip and Levy, Sidney J. (1969) 'Broadening the Concept of Marketing', *Journal of Marketing* 33 (January): 10–15.

Prahalad, C.K. (2004) *The Fortune at the Bottom of the Pyramid*, Engelwood Cliffs, NJ: Wharton School Publishing.

Rouse, W.H.D. (trans.) (1956) *Great Dialogues of Plato*, New York: Mentor. (Includes the *Republic*.)

Witzel, Morgen (2002) *Builders and Dreamers: The Making and Meaning of Management*, London: FT-Prentice Hall.

Witzel, Morgen (2012) *A History of Management Thought*, London: Routledge.

Bibliography

Akerlof, George A. (1970) 'The Market for Lemons: Quality Uncertainty and the Market Mechanism', *Quarterly Journal of Economics* 84 (3): 488–500.

Argyris, Chris (1957) *Personality and Organization*, New York: Harper & Row.

Arthur, W. Brian (1994), *Increasing Returns and Path Dependence in the Economy*, Ann Arbor, Michigan: University of Michigan Press.

Arvedlund, Erin (2009) *Too Good to Be True: The Rise and Fall of Bernie Madoff*, New York: Penguin Portfolio.

Babbage, Charles (1835) *The Economy of Machinery and Manufactures*, London: Charles Knight.

Baden-Fuller, Charles and Stopford, John (1992) *Rejuvenating the Mature Business*, London: Routledge.

Balch, Thomas Willing (2008) *The Law of Oresme, Copernicus and Gresham*, New York: Read.

Barnard, Chester I. (1938) *The Functions of the Executive*, Cambridge, MA: Harvard University Press.

Barwise, Patrick and Meehan, Seán (2011) *Beyond the Familiar: Long-term Growth Through Customer Focus and Innovation*, San Francisco: Jossey-Bass.

Bastiat, Frédéric (1850) *That Which Is Seen, and That Which Is Not Seen*, http://bastiat.org/ en/twisatwins.html.

Bateson, Gregory (1988) *Mind and Nature: A Necessary Unity*, New York: Bantam.

Bijapurkar, Rama (2008) *We Are Like That Only*, New Delhi: Penguin India.

Bird, Richard J. (2003) *Chaos and Life: Complexity and Order in Evolution and Thought*, Columbia: Columbia University Press.

Bose, R.N. (1956) *Gandhian Technique and Tradition in Industrial Relations*, Calcutta: All-India Institute of Social Welfare and Business Management.

Boulding, Kenneth (1956) *The Image*, Ann Arbor: University of Michigan Press.

Brock, David C. (2006) *Understanding Moore's Law: Four Decades of Innovation*, Philadelphia: Chemical Heritage Foundation.

Brocka, Bruce and Brocka, Suzanne (1992) *Quality Management: Implementing the Best Ideas of the Masters*, Homewood, IL: Business One Irwin.

Brodie, Morris B. (1967) *Fayol on Administration*, London: Lyon, Grant & Green.

Buffett, Warren and Cunningham, Lawrence A. (2008) *The Essays of Warren Buffett*, New York: John Wiley & Sons.

Carroll, Sean (2011) *From Eternity to Here: The Quest for the Ultimate Theory of Time*, New York: Oneworld Publications.

Chakravarthy, Bala and Lorange, Peter (2008) *Profit or Growth? Why You Don't Have to Choose*, Upper Saddle River, NJ: Wharton School Publishing.

Chandler, George (1964) *Four Centuries of Banking*, London: B.T. Batsford.

Chen Huan-Chang (1911) *The Economic Principles of Confucius and His School*, New York: Longmans, Green; repr. Bristol: Thoemmes Press, 2002, with an introduction by Morgen Witzel.

Christensen, Clayton (1997) *The Innovator's Dilemma: When New Technologies Cause Great Firms to Fail*, Boston: Harvard Business School Press.

Clausewitz, Karl von (1819) *Vom Kriege*, ed. and trans. Michael Howard and Peter Paret, *On War*, Princeton: Princeton University Press, 1984.

Crosby, Philip B. (1979) *Quality Is Free: The Art of Making Quality Certain*, New York: McGraw-Hill.

Darwin, Charles (2006) *On the Origin of Species by Means of Natural Selection*, Mineola, NY: Dover.

De Roover, Raymond (1949) *Gresham on Foreign Exchange*, Cambridge, MA: Harvard University Press.

Deming, W. Edwards (1986) *Out of the Crisis*, Cambridge, MA: MIT Center for Advanced Engineering Study.

Dixon, Norman (1976) *On the Psychology of Military Incompetence*, London: Pimlico.

Drucker, Peter F. (1954) *The Practice of Management*, New York: Harper & Row.

Drucker, Peter F. (1967) *The Effective Executive*, New York: Harper & Row.

Elkind, Peter and McLean, Bethany (2004) *The Smartest Guys in the Room: The Amazing Rise and Scandalous Fall of Enron*, New York: Penguin.

Emerson, Harrington (1909) *Efficiency as a Basis for Operations and Wages*, New York: John R. Dunlap.

Fayol, Henri (1984) *General and Industrial Management*, New York: David S. Lake.

Follett, Mary Parker (1924) *Creative Experience*, New York: Longmans, Green.

Forrester, Jay Wright (1961) *Industrial Dynamics*, Portland, OR: Productivity Press.

Foucault, Michel (1977) *Discipline and Punish: Birth of the Prison*, trans. Alan Sheridan, London: Allen Lane.

Gabor, Andrea (1990) *The Man Who Discovered Quality*, New York: Times Books.

Gerstner, Louis V. (2002) *Who Says Elephants Can't Dance?* New York: HarperCollins.

Greenleaf, Robert K. (1977) *Servant Leadership*, Mahwah, NJ: Paulist Press.

Greising, David (1998) *I'd Like the World to Buy a Coke: The Life and Leadership of Roberto Goizueta*, New York: John Wiley & Sons.

Grove, Andrew (1983) *High Output Management*, New York: Random House.

Grove, Andrew (1996) *Only the Paranoid Survive: How to Exploit the Crisis Points that Challenge Every Company and Career*, New York: HarperCollins.

Gulick, Luther H. and Urwick, Lyndall (1937) *Papers on the Science of Administration*, New York: Institute for Public Administration.

Hamel, Gary and Prahalad, C.K. (1994) *Competing for the Future*, Boston, MA: Harvard Business School Press.

Handy, Charles (1976) *Understanding Organisations*, London: Penguin.

Handy, Charles (1989) *The Age of Unreason*, London: Business Books.

Handy, Charles (1995) *The Empty Raincoat: Making Sense of the Future*, London: Arrow.

Herzberg, Frederick (1966) *Work and the Nature of Man*, Cleveland: World Publishing Company.

Hodgson, Geoffrey and Knudsen, Thorbjørn (2010) *Darwin's Conjecture: The Search for General Principles of Social and Scientific Evolution*, Chicago: University of Chicago Press.

Hughes, Patrick and Brecht, George (1975) *Vicious Circles and Infinity: A Panoply of Paradoxes*, Garden City, NY: Doubleday.

Ishikawa, Kaoru (1989) *Introduction to Quality Control*, London: Chapman & Hall.

Jarrett, Michael (2009) *Changeability: Why Some Companies Are Ready for Change – And Others Aren't*, London: FT-Prentice Hall.

Jay, Anthony (1967) *Management and Machiavelli*, London: Hodder & Stoughton.

Jevons, William Stanley (1866) *The Coal Question*, London: Macmillan.

Juran, Joseph M. and Gryna, Frank M. (1993) *Quality Planning and Analysis*, New York: McGraw-Hill.

Kanter, Rosabeth Moss (1989) *When Giants Learn to Dance*, New York: Simon & Schuster.

Kaynak, Erdener and Kahle, Lynn R. (2000) *Cross-national Consumer Psychographics*, London: Routledge.

Kemp, Jacques, Schotter, Andreas and Witzel, Morgen (2012) *Management Frameworks*, London: Routledge.

Kets de Vries, Manfred (2007) 'The Spirit of Despotism: Understanding the Tyrant Within', *Human Relations* 59 (2): 195–220.

Kloetzli, R. (2004) *Buddhist Cosmology: From Single World System to Pure Land*, Delhi: Motilal Banarsidass.

Kotler, Philip and Levy, Sidney J. (1969) 'Broadening the Concept of Marketing', *Journal of Marketing* 33 (January): 10–15.

Kropotkin, Peter (1976) *Mutual Aid: A Factor of Evolution*, New York: Sargent.

Kumar, Umesh (1990) *Kautilya's Thought on Public Administration*, New Delhi: National Book Organization.

Lao Tzu (1990), *Daodejing* (*Tao Teh Ching*), Boston: Shambhala.

Lau, D.C. (1979) *Confucius: The Analects*, Harmondsworth: Penguin.

Lepawski, Albert (1949) *Administration: The Art and Science of Organisation and Management*, New York: Alfred A. Knopf.

Lipman-Blumen, Jean (2004) *The Allure of Toxic Leaders: Why We Follow Destructive Bosses and Corrupt Politicians – And How We Can Survive Them*, Oxford: Oxford University Press.

Mackay, Charles (1995) *Extraordinary Popular Delusions and the Madness of Crowds*, London: Wordsworth.

Mah alanobis, P.C. (1948) 'Walter A. Shewhart and Statistical Control in India', *Sankhya: The Indian Journal of Statistics* 9 (1): 51–75.

March, James G. and Simon, Herbert A. (1958) *Organizations*, New York: John Wiley.

Maslow, Abraham (1954) *Motivation and Personality*, New York: Harper & Bros.

Mason, Paul (2008) *Live Working or Die Fighting: How the Working Class Went Global*, London: Vintage.

McGregor, Douglas (1960) *The Human Side of Enterprise*, New York: McGraw-Hill.

Merton, Robert K. (1936) 'The Unanticipated Consequences of Purposive Social Action', *American Sociological Review*, in Merton, *Sociological Ambivalence and Other Essays*, New York: Free Press, 1976.

Michels, Roberto (1949) *Political Parties: A Sociological Study of the Oligarchical Tendencies of Modern Democracy*, New York: Dover.

Mintzberg, Henry (1973) *The Nature of Managerial Work*, New York: Harper & Row.

Mintzberg, Henry and Quinn, James Brian (eds) (1988) *The Strategy Process*, Englewood Cliffs, NJ: Prentice Hall.

Nayar, Vineet (2010) *Employees First, Customers Second: Turning Conventional Management Upside Down*, Boston: Harvard Business School Press.

Ohmae, Kenichi (1982) *The Mind of the Strategist*, New York: McGraw-Hill.

Ohno, Taiichi (1988) *Toyota Production System: Beyond Large Scale Production*, Cambridge, MA: Productivity Press.

Parkinson, C. Northcote (1958) *Parkinson's Law*, London: John Murray.

Paul, Helen Julia (2010) *The South Sea Bubble: An Economic History of its Origins and Consequences*, London: Routledge.

Penrose, Roger (2005) *The Road to Reality: A Complete Guide to the Laws of the Universe*, New York: Alfred A. Knopf.

Peter, Laurence J. (1969) *The Peter Principle*, London: Pan.

Prahalad, C.K. (2004) *The Fortune at the Bottom of the Pyramid*, Engelwood Cliffs, NJ: Wharton School Publishing.

Refuge, Eustache de (2008) *Treatise on the Court*, trans. J. Chris Cooper, Boca Raton, FL: Orgpax Publications.

Rouse, W.H.D. (trans.) (1956) *Great Dialogues of Plato*, New York: Mentor.

Rudra, Ashok (1998) *Prasanta Chandra Mahalanobis: A Biography*, New Delhi: Oxford University Press.

Semler, Ricardo (1993) *Maverick! The Success Story Behind the World's Most Unusual Workplace*, London: Arrow.

Shea, Gary S. (2007) 'Understanding Financial Derivatives During the South Sea Bubble: The Case of the South Sea Subscription Shares', *Oxford Economic Papers* 59 (Supplement 1).

Sheth, Jagdish N. (2007) *The Self-destructive Habits of Good Companies, and How to Break Them*, Engelwood Cliffs, NJ: Wharton School Publishing.

Shiller, Robert J. (2005) *Irrational Exuberance*, Princeton: Princeton University Press.

Siedel, George and Haapio, Helena (2010) *Proactive Law for Managers*, Farnham: Gower.

Strassman, W. Paul (1990) *The Business Value of Computers*, New Canaan, CT: Information Economics Press.

Sull, Donald N. (2003) *Why Good Companies Go Bad, and How Great Managers Remake Them*, Boston: Harvard Business School Press.

Sunzi (1963) *The Art of War*, trans. L. Giles, ed. Samuel B. Griffiths, Oxford: Oxford University Press.

Taylor, Frederick Winslow (1911) *The Principles of Scientific Management*, New York: Harper & Bros; repr. Stilwell, KS: Digireads.com.

Triana, Pablo (2009) *Lecturing Birds on Flying: Can Mathematical Theories Destroy the Financial Markets?* Chichester: John Wiley.

Urwick, Lyndall (1937) 'The Function of Administration', in Luther Gulick and Lyndall Urwick (eds), *Papers on the Science of Administration*, New York: Institute of Public Administration.

Vasconcellos e Sá, Jorge (2005) *Strategy Moves*, London: Pearson Education.

Wallace, Alfred Russel (2008) *Darwinism*, New York: Macmillan.

Weisman, Stewart L. (1999) *Need and Greed: The Story of the Largest Ponzi Scheme in American History*, Syracuse, NY: Syracuse University Press.

Whicker, Marcia Lynn (1996) *Toxic Leaders: When Organizations Go Bad*, Westport, CT: Quorum Books.

Witzel, Morgen (2002) *Builders and Dreamers: The Making and Meaning of Management*, London: FT-Prentice Hall.

Witzel, Morgen (2010) *Tata: The Evolution of a Corporate Brand*, New Delhi: Penguin Portfolio.

Witzel, Morgen (2012) *A History of Management Thought*, London: Routledge.

Womack, James P., Jones, Daniel T., and Roos, Daniel (1990) *The Machine That Changed the World*, New York: Macmillan

Index